new trends in house design

Thomas Hanrahan & Victoria
Jn Studio Van Berkel & Bos Matthe
Joy Graham Phillips Tadao Ando P
Norman Foster & Partners J.
Mark Guard Wiel Arets Ric
Camagna Camoletto
Clifford + Thompson
Ishiguro Christophe L
Collin Architect Claus
Studio John Pawson
Klotz Legorreta Ar
Conder & A
Koolhaas R
tecture Us
Beneder Ian
Semba Dav
Freie Archit
Hammer & Lassen H

eyers Fraser Brown MacKenna Priestman Architects MVRDV Rick er W. Schmidt Claudio Silvestrin Sir Martínez Lapeña & Elías Torres ard Rogers Partnership Waro Kishi arcante ARCHITECTUS: Bowes, ol Eduardo Souto de Moura Koichiro Engelen Moore Shigeru Ban Arthur Kaan José Cruz Ovalle Moneo Brock Alvaro Siza Koh Kitayama Mathias itectos Behnisch & Partner Simon ociates Mario Botta LOG ID Rem aplan TEN Arquitectos GAD archi- da Findlay Partnership Ernst Hay Kunihide Oshinomi & Takeshi Adjaye Associates Bürlingschindler kten BDA Architekten Schmidt, s Kollhoff Legorreta Arquitectos K.

new **trends** *in* **house** *design*

Special edition for:

Gingko Press GmbH
Hamburger Strasse 180
D-22083 Hamburg
Germany

Phone: +49 (0)40 - 291 425
Fax: +49 (0)40 - 291 055
e-mail: gingkopress@t-online.de

Gingko Press Inc.
5768 Paradise Drive, Suite J
Corte Madera, CA 94925
USA

Phone: +1 - 415 - 924 9615
Fax: +1 - 415 - 924 9608
e-mail: books@gingkopress.com
www.gingkopress.com

Work conception: Carles Broto
Publisher: Arian Mostaedi

Graphic design & production: Pilar Chueca & Héctor Navarro
Text: Contributed by the architects, edited
*   by Jacobo Krauel and Amber Ockrassa*

© Carles Broto i Comerma
Jonqueres, 10, 1-5
08003 Barcelona, Spain
Tel.: +34 93 301 21 99 Fax: +34-93-301 00 21
E-mail: info@linksbooks.net

ISBN: 1-58423-193-9

Printed in Spain

new trends in house design

Gingko Press

There are trend setters and there are trend followers. Trend setters rewrite the old rules that trend followers then obey. It is the trend setters that we were looking for in putting together this collection. We were looking for new interpretations, fresh viewpoints, innovations. In short, we were looking for designs that are destined to determine the future of architecture. The results of our search are varied.

See, for example, Koh Kitayama's masterful reinterpretation of traditional Japanese architecture in the Omni Quarter project. Or Norman Foster's artistry in working with glass and steel in a house in Germany. In the Film House project, Christophe Lab ingeniously creates light and space where none previously existed. The list goes on.

Since technical know-how is just as important as artistic vision in any project, we have touched upon every aspect in the design and construction processes to give a well-rounded vision. From conception to completion, we have included information on material and construction processes in order to complement the design ideas of the contributing architects. Finally, since nobody is in a better position to comment on these projects than the designers themselves, we have included the architects' own comments and anecdotes.

Therefore, we trust that we are leaving you in good, expert hands and that this selection of some of the finest, most innovative architectural solutions in the world will serve as an endless source of inspiration. Enjoy!

Tadao Ando
House in Nihonbashi

Osaka, Japan

Located in the fluorishing Osaka commercial district of Minami, the area is composed of a confused mixture of shops, restaurants and old residential buildings. Though disorganized, the cityscape is charged with a chaotic urban energy that is truly Osakan.

As is cornmon in the area, the site has a narrow frontage and is deeply recessed. The building, with an exceedingly narrow plan of 2.9 x 15 meters, stands four stories high and is sandwiched between the neighboring buildings.

A store occupies the first floor, with the second to fourth levels used as residences. Two vertical voids divide the slender, deeply recessed plan. One -a double-volume exterior space on the third and fourth levels- is reached by ascending a narrow staircase from the building's entrance. This outdoor space, set in the middle of the residence, allows light to spill down into the narrowly confined living area, while forming a breezy court and framing a segment of the sky.

The other void is the large space of the living room, which runs vertically through three levels of the residence, from the second to the fourth floor. Separated by no more than a single plane of frosted glazing from the chaotic urban surroundings, this void faces the road. These two voids of different qualities run through the single, mono-functional space of the house in a crevice-like manner. All the rooms face these crevices and the occupants must come and go by means of them. Through these crevices each room receives the presence of nature and the vitality of the city, thus ensuring a dwelling space of richness and variety.

Photographs: Tomio Ohashi

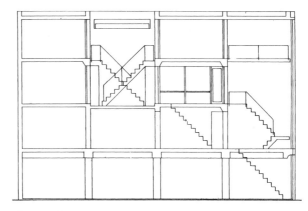

Cross section

Site plan

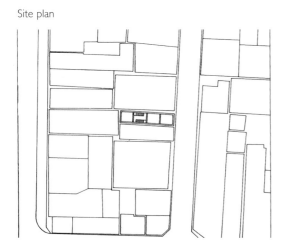

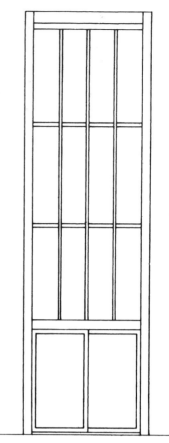

Main elevation

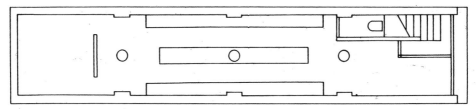

Ground floor plan

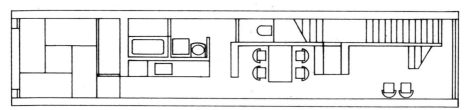

First floor plan

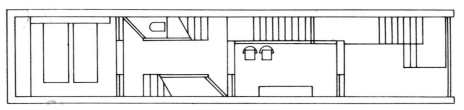

Second floor plan

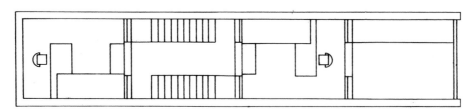

Third floor plan

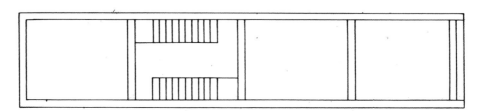

Roof plan

The dwelling has been adapted to the dimensions of a deep and narrow site (2.9x 15 meters) located in a district of frenetic commercial activity in the city of Osaka.
The architect has made use of the narrowness of the site, conceiving double-height spaces that heighten the sensation of extreme verticality in the home's interior.
The wide living-room is protected from the chaotic Osaka's urban organization by a single plane of frosted glazing.

Sir Norman Foster & Partners
Private House

Germany

This is a house for a young family with small children. The building is sited on a southfacing slope, which is well wooded and enjoys fine views of the valley beyond.

Access to the site from the road is directly on to the roof terrace of the house, which is a two story concrete and brickwork structure dug into the hillside. From this level an entrance ramp leads down through the levels of the house to the lower garden terrace. Both of these outdoor spaces are protected by a louvered roof with its own independent steel structure.

The lowest level is the family domain, which contains the booklined hearth and the open kitchen. Both areas are adjacent to the double height living space. One of the central features of the house is its splendid kitchen. The owner has a personal interest in cooking, which is reflected in the professional appliances and a very efficient extraction system.

All levels of the dwelling are connected by exterior steps in the landscape. These allow direct access to the garden for children, quiet outdoor spaces overlooked by the parents´ study and a private front door for the maid.

The design, based on an unusual combination of inside and outside circulation, provides the family and their friends with an unusual degree of community as well as respecting the privacy of the individuals.

Photographs: Dennis Gilbert

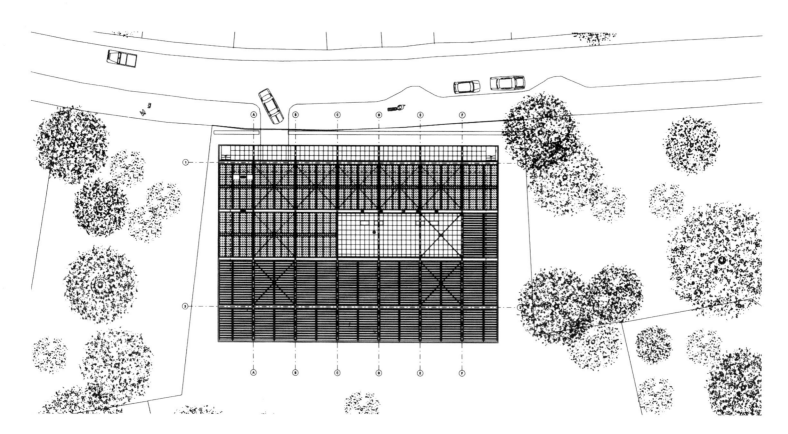

Upper level floor plan

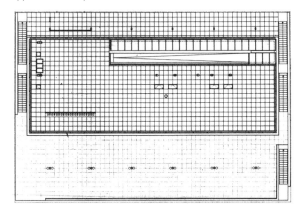

First floor plan

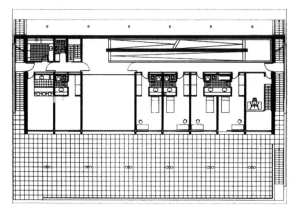

Ground floor plan

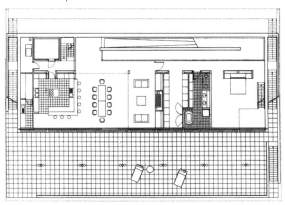

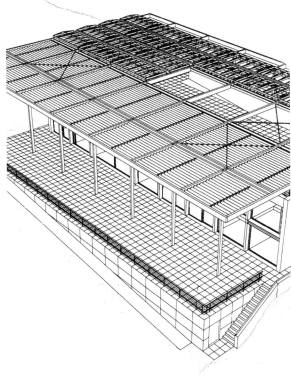

The external appearance of the building is dominated by a large lattice supported by an independent metal structure.

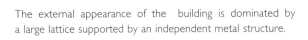

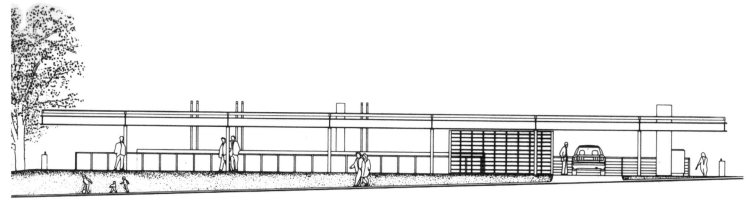

North elevation

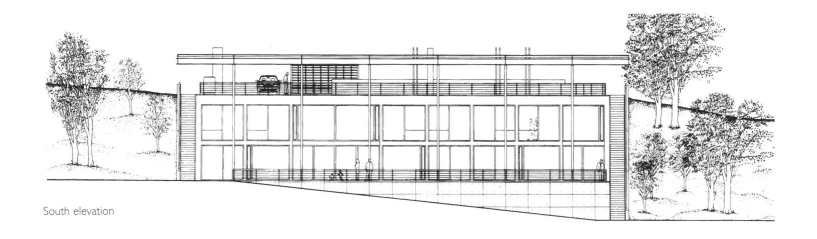

South elevation

Moneo Brock Studio
Tribeca Home and Studio

New York City, USA

The space lies on the two top floors of an 1898 warehouse building in Tribeca in New York City. The difficulties presented by the space in its original form were its low ceiling height, its triangular plan, its tight column grid, and the presence of low-hanging pipes throughout the space. The positive attributes presented by the space were excellent views, exclusive access to the roof, as well as the option to add skylights to provide light, air and a sense of greater openness. The 14" x 14" posts of white oak and 8" x 12" beams of yellow pine were also recognized as assets effusing an air of stout solidity.

In the plan the architects attempted to preserve as much as possible the feeling of open space found in the existing conditions; indeed, by opening the roof in strategic locations, that feeling was accentuated, providing, at the same time, the amenities required for living. Part of the strategy was to keep interventions clear of the columns and leave them on view, allowing the continuity of the structure to remain explicit and to thereby carry a sense of openness and fluidity of space.

The central column line, with its major north-south beam, naturally divides the space in two. The area to the east of this line was designated as a studio space, and the entry was moved to the west side of the line. The entry path parallel to the column line emphasizes the strength of the structure moving throughout the space, while maximizing the useful area in the studio. Over the studio area existed a large north-facing skylight that gave volume to the space. This was cleaned up and painted a warm yellow.

The area to the west of the column line was designated as living space. An existing roof opening to the south of this area was moved northward to sit directly over a module of the column grid, and a tall skylight with south-facing glass constructed atop. In the south glass of this skylight are operable windows and a door giving access to the roof deck. Furthermore, a folding aluminum stair with a landing made of glass tiles gives access to the high windows and the door. Over the living area, recesses were built into the ceiling wherever the spacing of the joists allowed. In these recesses, lights were placed behind planes of diffusing plexiglass to illuminate the room without glare, free from protruding elements below the ceiling surface. Over the entry hall, a similar construction gives a diffuse, general light.

The rooms requiring fixed connexions to the plumbing stack and/or solid enclosure for privacy (the kitchen, the two bathrooms and the bedroom) are constructed in a block to the west of the entry path which was designed to appear as an independent volume, like a large, fixed furniture piece. The block has been kept away from the exterior brick walls and the central column line, and encloses just one column.

Photographs: Michael Moran

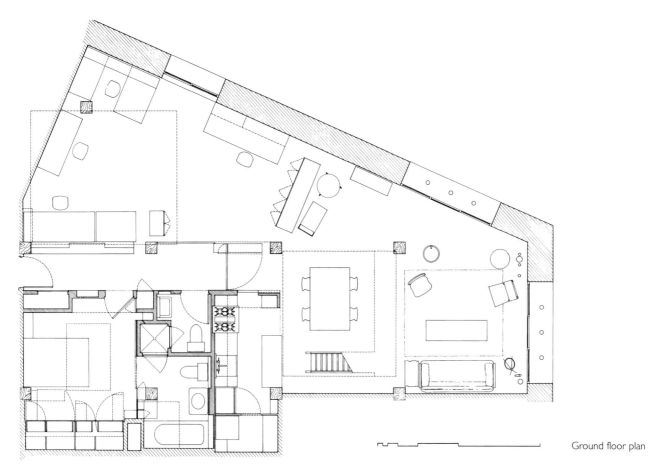

Ground floor plan

The stairway to the roof deck is rigged to a counterweight and can be lifted easily overhead to clear space in the living area. The glass floor is supported by a structure composed of a 6" steel channel as main beam and nine 2" T and two 2" angle sections as subsidiary supports. The steel sections are painted aluminum to match the stair, which is a prefabricated ship's ladder.

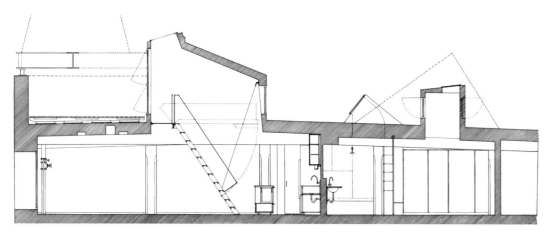

Longitudinal section

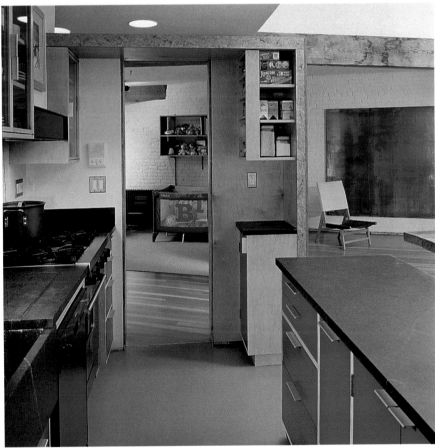

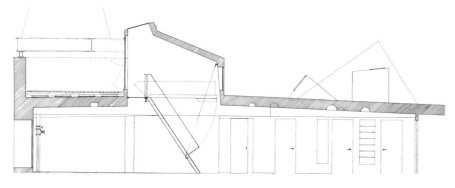

Longitudinal section

What most excited the architects about the living area skylight was that one of the building's rooftop water tanks was also brought into view by the placement of the glass wall high above the floor of the loft, giving the vertical dimension extra emphasis.

Public and private spaces are differentiated both stucturally and visually. The oriented strandboard used to clad the walls of the block composed of bedroom, bathrooms and kitchen sharply contrasts with the wooden posts and beams and gives the loft an industrial appearance.

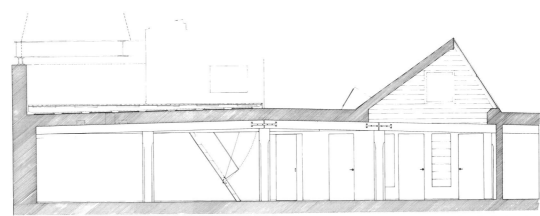

Longitudinal section

Graham Phillips
Skywood House

Middlessex, UK

The plot, etched into a densely populated zone, was subject to zoning laws which restricted the surface area available for construction to 250 m². The architect set out to create a "glass box" in the forest, a structure whose boundaries between interior and exterior would be blurred, where water would play a leading role. The house, lying before the shores of a lake, is reached via a black gravel walkway which winds around the house, ending at the main patio at the back. The building rests on a grey limestone plinth, its bare, unadorned surface highlighting its simple shapes. Frameless glass doors covered by a pergola, a design echoed in the entrance to the garage, form the main entryway. A noteworthy element in the exterior space is the main chimney, which hides the drainage system, the pipes and the ventilation system within a single unit. The dwelling is unified by long, 3-meter-high walls which reach beyond the enclosed spaces toward the lake and surrounding terrain, thereby defining footpaths. This minimalist expression contrasts with the wealth of the landscape, creating a serene and wondrous experience.

The dwelling is enclosed by two glass wings, the first of which, at a height of 3 meters, forms the volume containing the four bedrooms and their respective bathrooms. This module comprises one of the sides of a completely enclosed garden, which has a square lawn lying over a border of black gravel.

The glass volume which houses the sitting room is the tallest, thereby highlighting the steel sheet which comprises the floating roof. The main space enjoys breathtaking views across the lake to the west, toward the island, becoming as much a focal point by night as by day.

The tiling of the sitting room continues outward toward the garden, through a glass facade, blurring the boundaries between interior and exterior. This space is organized like a double square: the sitting room is defined by a 3.6 m² carpet centered over limestone flooring, a motif —that of a square framed within another background— which is seen again in the inside patio and the garden at the back. In the kitchen/dining room, a combination of sliding panels and two moveable tables allow a distribution which can be altered according to its users' needs.

Photographs: Nigel Young

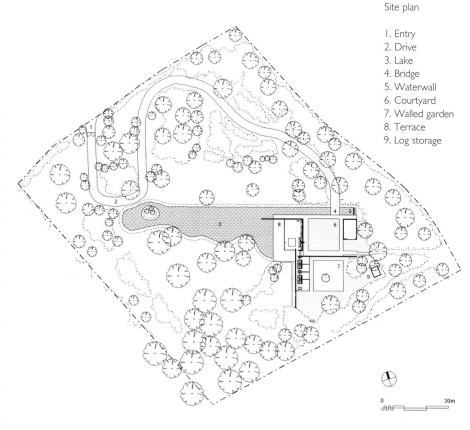

Site plan

1. Entry
2. Drive
3. Lake
4. Bridge
5. Waterwall
6. Courtyard
7. Walled garden
8. Terrace
9. Log storage

0   30m

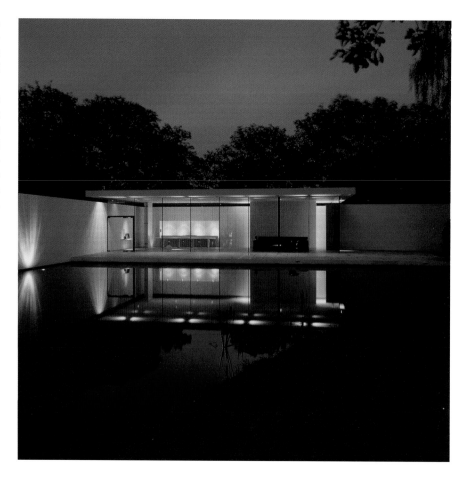

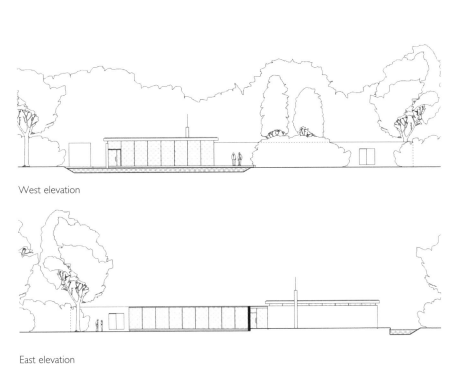

West elevation

East elevation

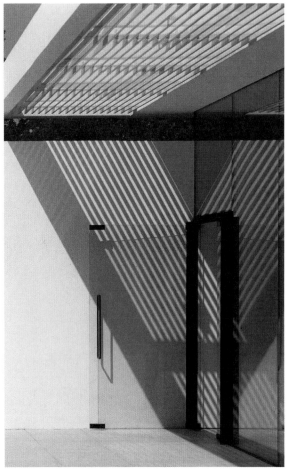

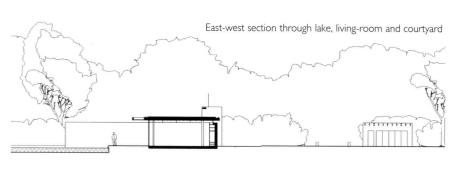

East-west section through lake, living-room and courtyard

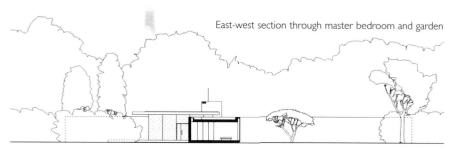

East-west section through master bedroom and garden

Ground floor plan

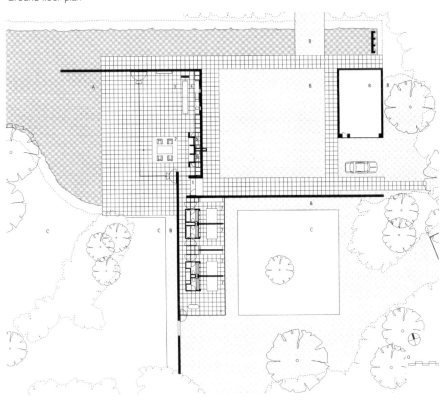

Limestone and glass, used both inside and out, confer homogeneity on the building and continuity between the exterior and interior. The entirety of the water, electrical and ventilation systems are operated through a single vertical duct, while the heating system is under the floor, thereby avoiding the need for radiators. The furniture and other decorative elements have been custom-designed for this home.

Construction detail

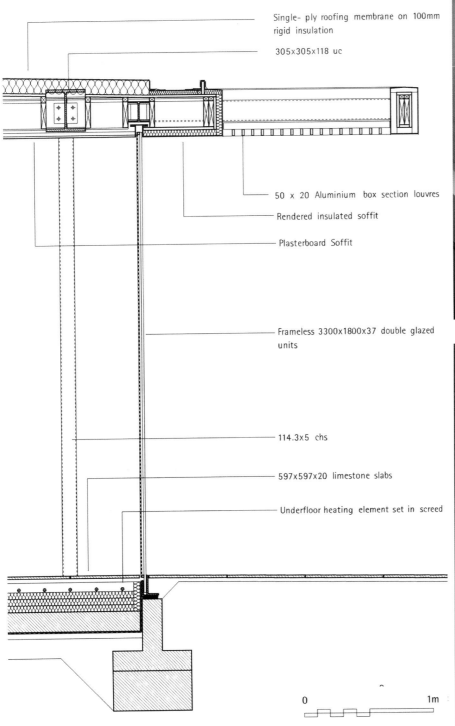

Single- ply roofing membrane on 100mm rigid insulation

305x305x118 uc

50 x 20 Aluminium box section louvres

Rendered insulated soffit

Plasterboard Soffit

Frameless 3300x1800x37 double glazed units

114.3x5 chs

597x597x20 limestone slabs

Underfloor heating element set in screed

0   1m

Eduardo Souto de Moura
Baião House

Baião, Portugal

For the Baião House the request of the client was to build a small residence for the weekends by restoring the old ruins of a previous building. The basic line of the project was to highlight and consolidate the remains of the old building, maintaining them as a walled garden, and to build the house completely separate.

The work began with the demolition of the supporting main wall and with the excavation for the preparation of the plot to situate the house. The house itself is a block of cement sunken into the land but open towards the River Douro. The program required a "Portuguese house", respecting the beauty of the landscape. In this case, the integration was achieved by the fact that the dwelling is very concealed; indeed, it almost appears to be buried in the surrounding terrain.

Despite the limited budget, it was possible to use materials from all over Europe: French aluminum profiles, Swiss building materials, Belgian guttering, Spanish sanitary appliances and Italian marbles and lamps, all without forgetting local materials: some pieces from the demolitions in Barredo, rubblework from Leira and elements of woodwork from Paredes. A combination and union of elements from all over the EU come together in this small holiday residence.

Photographs: Luis Ferreira Alves

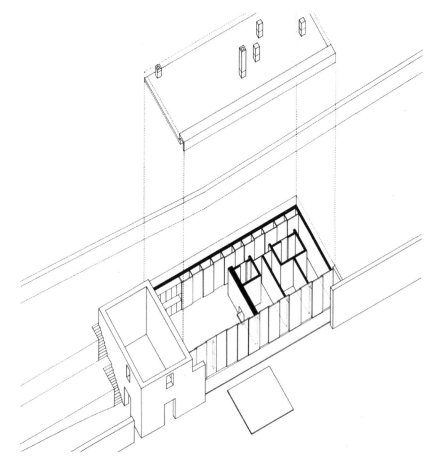

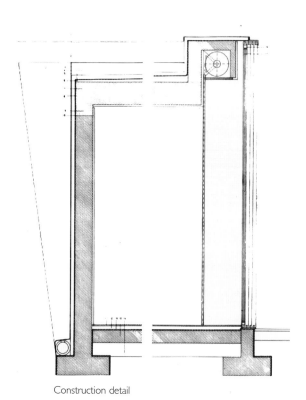

Construction detail

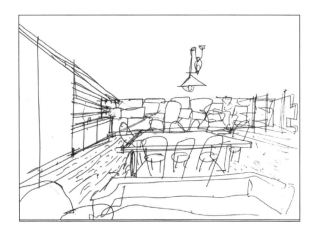

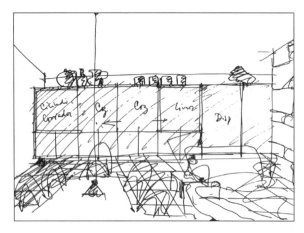

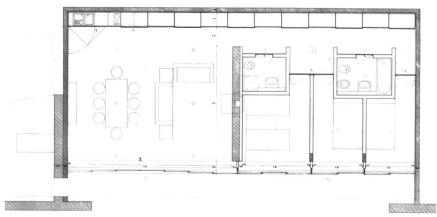

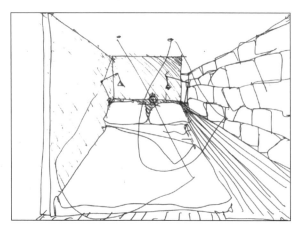

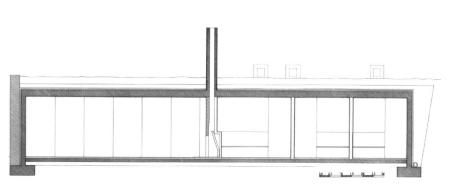

A stone wall belonging to the old ruins separates the area of the living-dining room and kitchen from the bedrooms and toilets. These two environments are communicated longitudinally by a rear corridor, with cupboards with sliding wooden doors, and opens toward the garden through sliding glass doors.

Mathias Klotz
Grau House

Santiago de Chile, Chile

Casa Grau is the result of the renovation of a house in a residential zone in Santiago dating from the 1950s.

The client originally wished to modify the access to the house and the stairs leading to the second floor. In the end, 70% of the building was demolished, leaving the floor slab between the first and second floor and the structural walls.

The scheme consisted of adding a third floor to house the main bedroom, leaving the second floor for the children and the first for the public space and the services. The original volume was clad in white stucco in contrast with the larger new volume.

For the new volume, a metal structure was used to create a vertical plane that crosses the whole house lengthwise, forming the access toward the street and the terrace roof facing the garden. This plane folds to form the ceiling, and the three remaining sides are glazed. This element forms the basis for the layout of the house.

The outside wall was clad in corrugated copper plate and, inside, with maniu wood panels.

The copper was given a green patina to produce a contrast with the original volume, and to complement the crowns of the trees.

The corrugated plate attenuates the deformations due to expansion and helps to create a regular texture.

The garden was designed by Juan Grimm, who created a large courtyard with vegetation, thus linking nature and artifice in a single environment.

Photographs: Mathias Klotz Studio

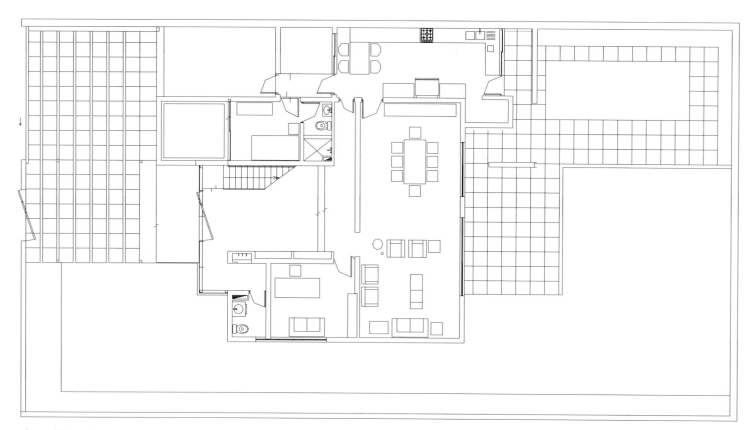

Ground floor plan

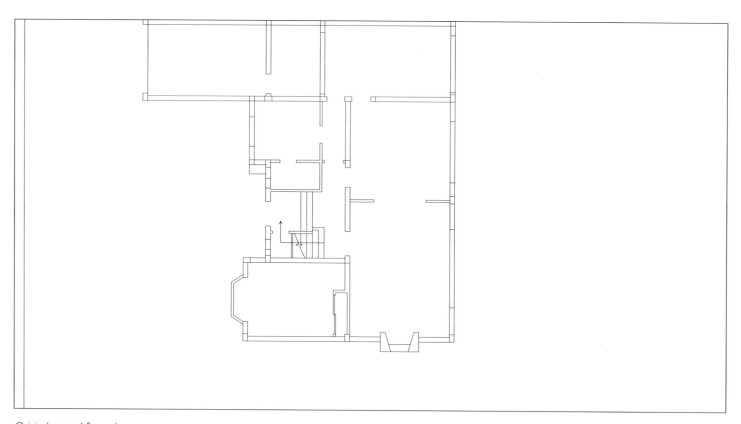

Original ground floor plan

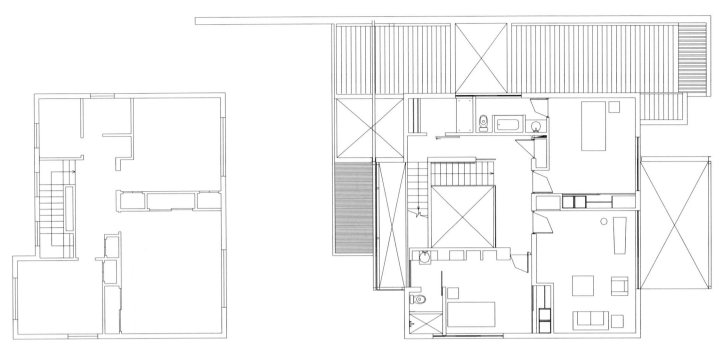

Original first floor plan

First floor plan

While 70% of the previous construction was demolished, the structural walls and floor slab between the first and second floors were retained. The interior of the new plane which crosses the house is clad in maniu wood.

Second floor plan

0   2m

A metal structure was used to create a vertical plane that crosses the house lengthwise, forming the access toward the street. This plane folds to form the ceiling, and the three remaining sides are glazed. The exterior wall is clad in copper, which was given a green patina.

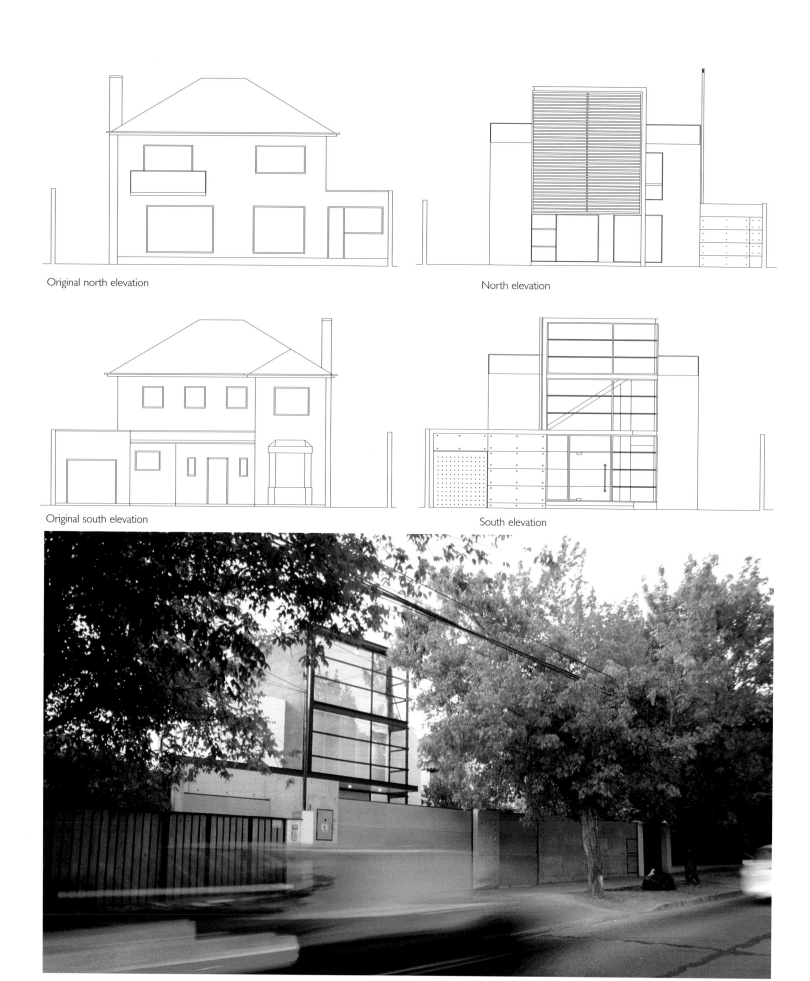

Original north elevation

North elevation

Original south elevation

South elevation

Original west elevation

0   2m

West elevation

Mario Botta
House in Daro-Bellinzona

Daro, Switzerland

The architecture of Mario Botta is characterized by its formal power and the strong presence of its volumes. His buildings do not attempt to blend into their surroundings; rather, they aim to impose themselves on them, to implant themselves with all the vigor of their architectural mass and become landmarks in the landscape. The single-family dwelling analyzed here is a clear example of this. It is located in the Swiss canton of Ticino, but is not subordinated to its Alpine setting. Instead, it makes use of the relief of the site to emerge with force, seeking to make a plastic, expressive impact.

The house in Daro abstains from Alpine typology and places all its visual power not in volume but in what amounts to a single facade which acts as a formal and visual point of reference for the whole project. All the expressive force of the building is concentrated on this facade, and is formalized in a wall with a fragmented design. The wall, which includes the main entrance, is defined by two characteristic features: the singular arrangement of the gray cement blocks in squares, which produce a variety of effects in the sunlight; and the transparent domed roof which crowns the building, giving it, in the words of Sergio Polano, the air of a "sun temple of an unknown civilization".

From the starting point of this facade, the building is laid out volumetrically to form a three-story body reminiscent of the keel of a ship embedded in the ground. A fourth level, in the basement, takes advantage of the slope of the land to create an extension to the floor plan, which is used as the garage and service area.

Photographs: Pino Musi

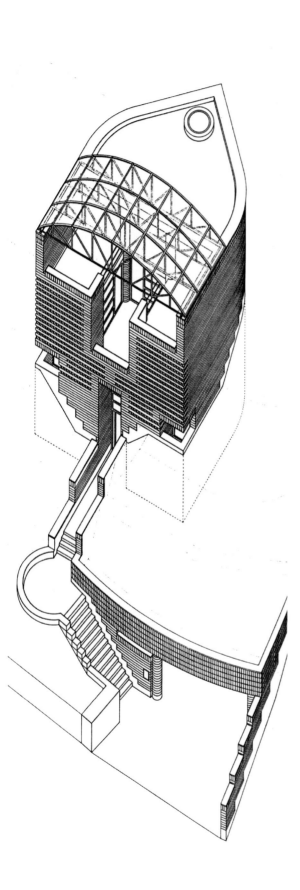

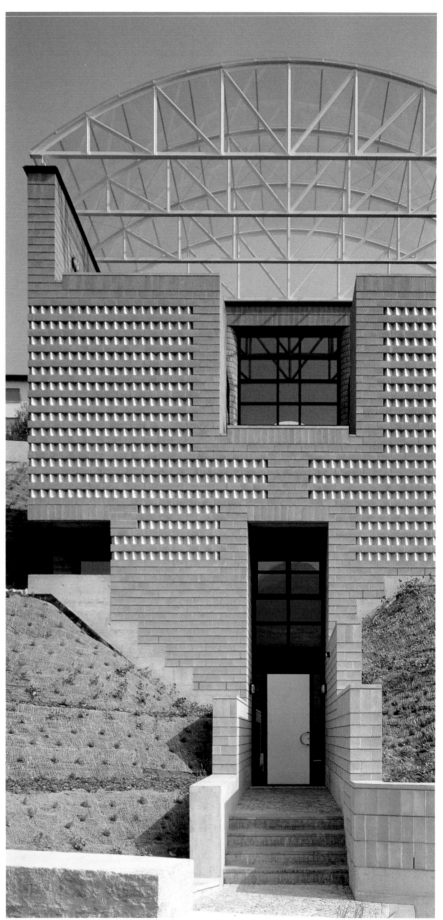

49

Second floor plan

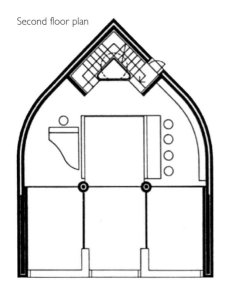

First floor plan

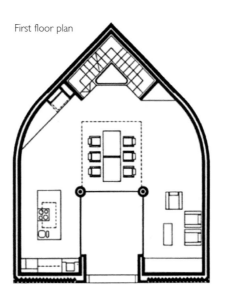

Ground floor plan

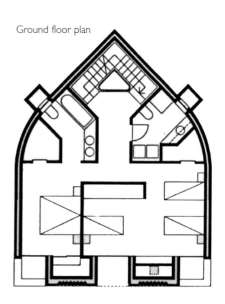

Basement floor plan

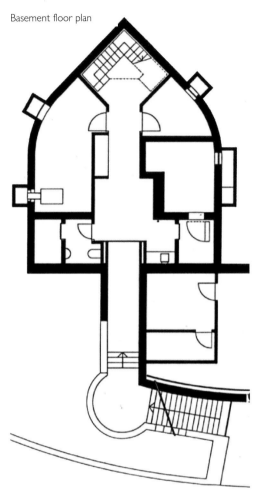

Shigeru Ban
2/5 House

West Japan

The 15x25 m rectangular plan of this house is divided into five zones each of 15x5 m. From the south these zones are: front garden, interior space, central courtyard, interior space, back garden. The house is bounded on its east and west sides by two-story reinforced concrete walls.

In order to create the 2/5 (i.e. 2 by 1/5) first floor space, enclosed glass boxes, similar to that of the Mies' Farnsworth House, were positioned across the second floor. The spaces created beneath these have a Japanese sensibility in which interior and exterior are linked both visually and physically. This contrasts with the merely visual spatial connectivity of Mies' work.

The first floor is a "universal floor": a unified space within which each of the functional elements is placed, while at the same time the use of sliding doors at the boundary between interior and exterior, and the manually operated tent roof results in a sense both of enclosure and openness.

The screen on the road side is formed from bent, punched aluminum which folds up accordion-like to form the garage door. On the north side a grid of PVC gutters have been hung as planters, creating a dense screen which ensures privacy.

Photographs: Hiroyuki Hirai

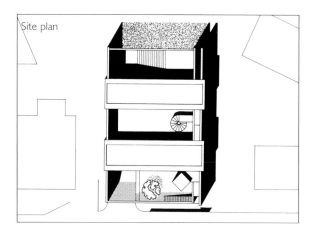

Site plan

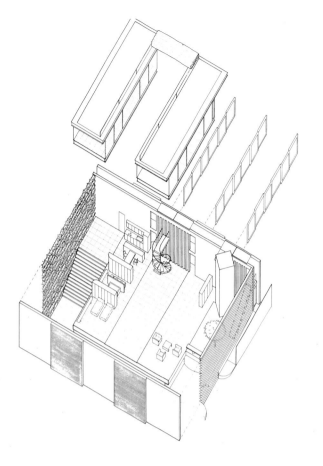

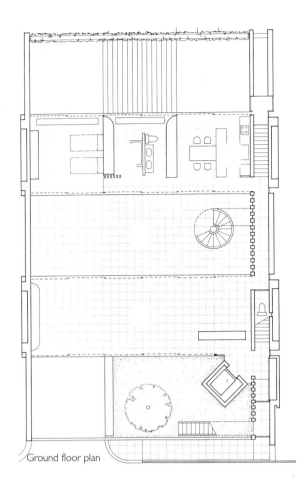

Ground floor plan

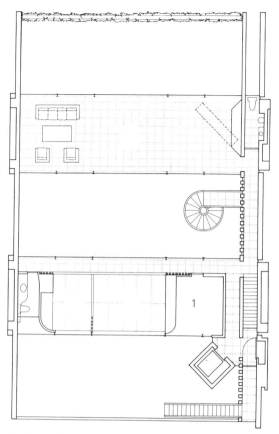

First floor plan

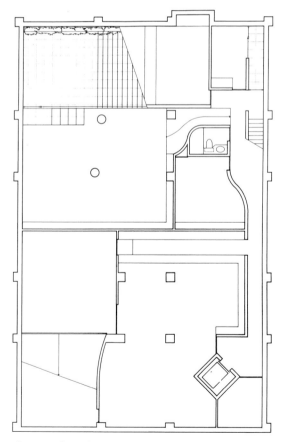

Basement floor plan

The street-side facade of the dwelling is clad in a sheet of perforated corrugated metal that offers a high degree of privacy and creates a special visual connection with the exterior.

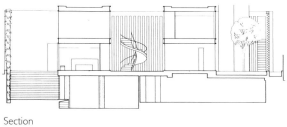

Section

The combination of open and closed spaces on the two floors results in dynamic atmospheres that are visually connected and adapt easily to the different uses that the residents may require in the future.

Richard Meier
Rachofksy House

Dallas, USA

Set in a suburban landscape, this house/private museum is anchored to the ground by a podium clad in black granite that extends both in front of and behind the main body of the building. The white form of the house hovers on piles above the podium like an opaque plane, pierced by a number of discrete openings. A succession of spatial layers recedes from this surface to accommodate the house's principal volumes. The metal-faced front elevation that shields the living volume gives way on the north and west elevations to taut curtain walls that, together with the opaque front, reflect the interior layered space toward a small body of water to the southwest. Two sheets of water -a reflection pool and a swimming pool- penetrate the podium at the rear of the house. The swimming pool, plus a cube-shaped poolhouse and a low wall, effectively terminate the sitework at the western end.

Two separate stairs provide access to the three floors of the house; an enclosed spiral stair to the south and an open switch-back stair to the north. This contrast between private and public circulation is echoed consistently in the organization of the volumes within. Thus, the public stair opening off the gallery foyer leads directly to the double-height living room on the first floor, while the cylindrical private stair ascends to the guest suite and library on the second floor and the master suite on the floor above. Two separate volumes on the third floor, a suspended study and an excercise room, afford views of the living volume and the garden. All glass walls that are exposed to low-angle western light are protected by electrically operated venetian blinds.

A ramped stair giving access from the swimming pool, a dog-leg stair to the roof terrace, and a two-car garage lodged under the guest suite on the south side of the house complete the symmetrical repertoire. The exterior of the house is clad in white enameled aluminum panels with aluminum fenestration and insulated glazing.

Photographs: Scott Frances / ESTO Photographics

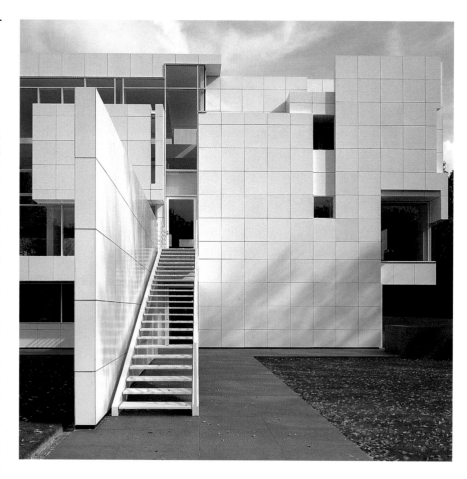

The stairways set the pace for both the building's interior and exterior. A metal structure following the progression of the wall provides access from the garden.

Site plan

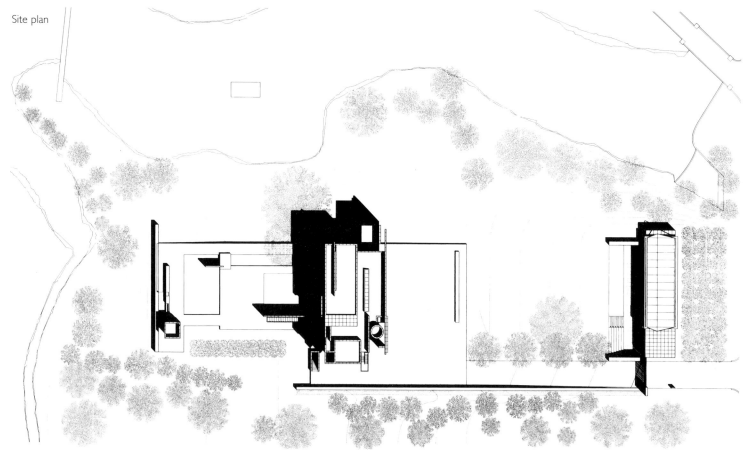

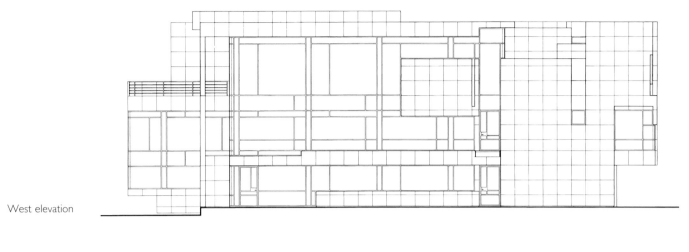

West elevation

Section to the west

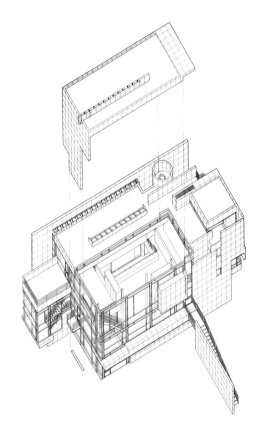

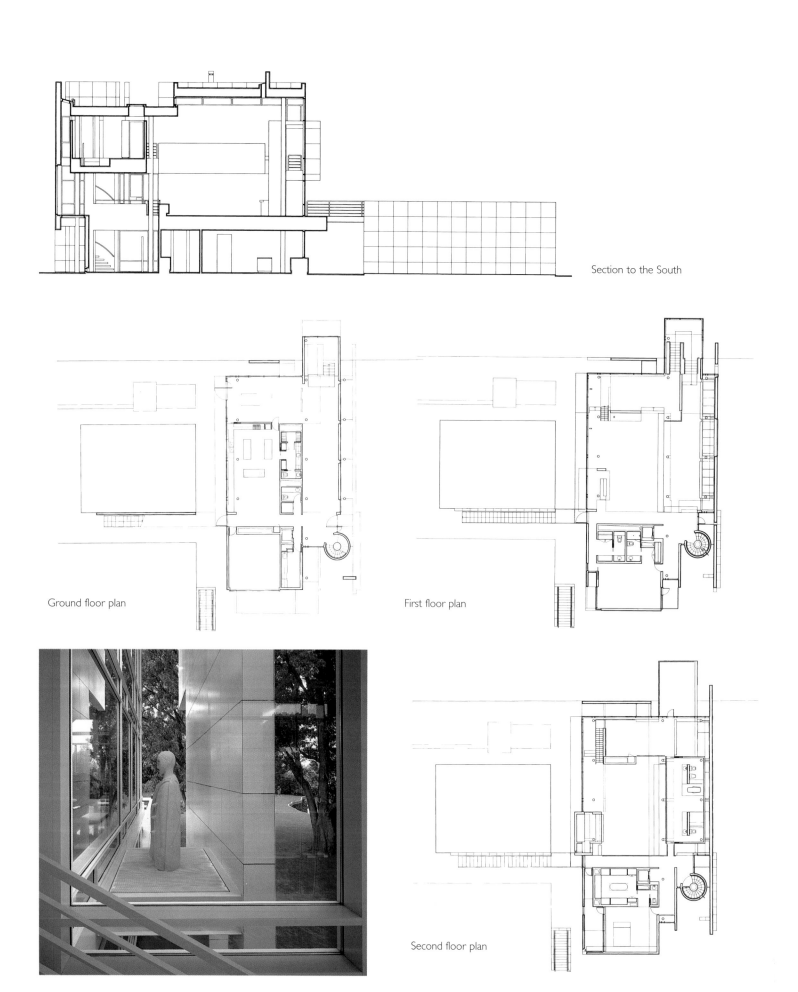

Section to the South

Ground floor plan

First floor plan

Second floor plan

63

Scogim, Elam & Bray
Mountain House

Dillard, Georgia, USA

From the galleries and studios of the city, he collects regional art with the same care and affection that she gathers the wildflowers of their north Georgia site. The site and the house respond to dual interests. The site -remote, private and rugged- is tucked into the foothills of the Appalachian Mountains overlooking the pasture of the Hambridge Center, a non-profit artists' retreat.

At the house the screened-in porch vies with the living room for prominence. The two spaces, outdoor/indoor, reside in a state of balance, happily. The generous arrival courtyard, square and stone-clad, spills into the vertical space of the entrance gallery and visually into the corridor gallery. It is the first interior space of the house.

The structure aspires to sustain a dialogue about the relationship between the natural and the human-made and the joys and wonders of both. Horizontal lines slice the round, softly arching and curving mountain forms. Wonderfully vertical poplar trunks are frame cut, celebrated. Used now as a weekend retreat, the house will eventually become the main residence. A small guest room detached from the house provides privacy and community.

The house proper has one bedroom. Building area: 4095 square feet. The frame is wood and steel with reinforced concrete walls defining and punctuating the rectilinear geometry. The house is clad in stucco, redwood and glass. The windows are redwood, the doors are mahogany, and the flooring is wood. The entrance courtyard is paved with rock pulled from a stream.

Photographs: Timothy Hursley

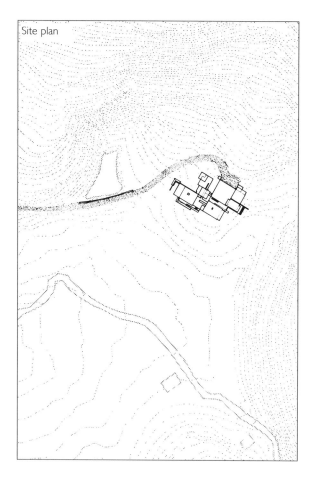

Site plan

The single-story dwelling is arranged to form a square courtyard, which then becomes another living space, reinforcing the idea of dialogue and interrelation between interior and exterior.

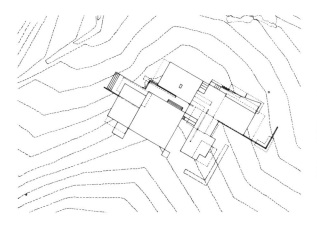

The project is defined by the highly horizontal geometry of the construction. Besides suggesting the interior program -rational and practical division, spaciousness and a great sensation of freedom-, the horizontal lines establish a dialogue with the vertical trunks of the surrounding trees. The relationship with the landscape is not mimetic but compensatory.

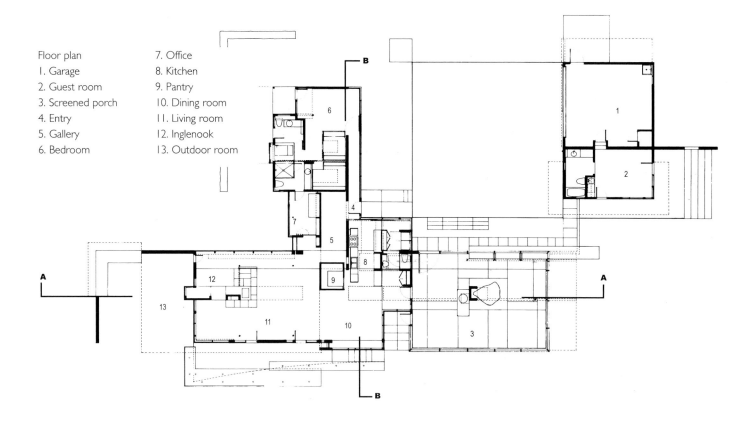

Floor plan
1. Garage
2. Guest room
3. Screened porch
4. Entry
5. Gallery
6. Bedroom
7. Office
8. Kitchen
9. Pantry
10. Dining room
11. Living room
12. Inglenook
13. Outdoor room

The glazed porch is a fundamental element of the dwelling. Its structure of wooden posts and beams has been left exposed, in an artificial recreation of the exterior forest.

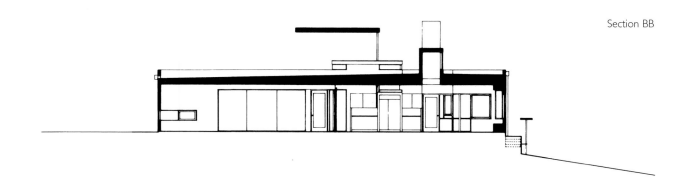

Section BB

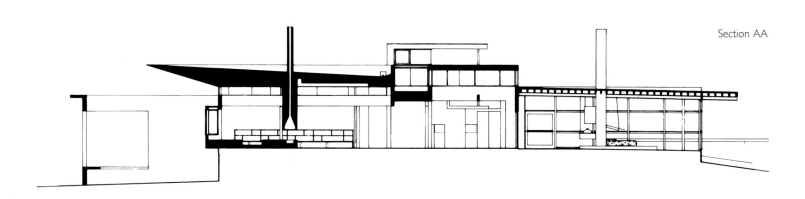

Section AA

Legorreta Arquitectos
House in Monte Tauro

México DF, Mexico

This house was designed to meet the requirements of a single person to enjoy contemporary life in an urban atmosphere. The client often uses his car, so the garage was highlighted by making its form part of the hall. By means of ingenious platforms it is possible to park four cars, two above and two below.

The central space overlooks a courtyard with a fountain, a tree and red earth paving, which offers the perfect atmosphere for conversation, reading, work and eating outdoors in a flexible and private environment.

A narrow staircase leads to a small gym that looks like a courtyard with a narrow glazed corridor and enjoys a view of trees and the street. This space is suitable for exercise, a swim, a shower or a bath. The four walls of the bedroom are covered with shelves and cupboards full of books and objects of daily use, the bed and the reading sofa. The natural and artificial light offers a variety of effects through the lamps and the painted windows. No element is decorative in this dwelling. All the objects are part of their owner's daily life. Space, color and light have been used to create a romantic and spiritual retreat that protects the occupant from the chaotic urban life of a large city.

Photographs: Lourdes Legorreta

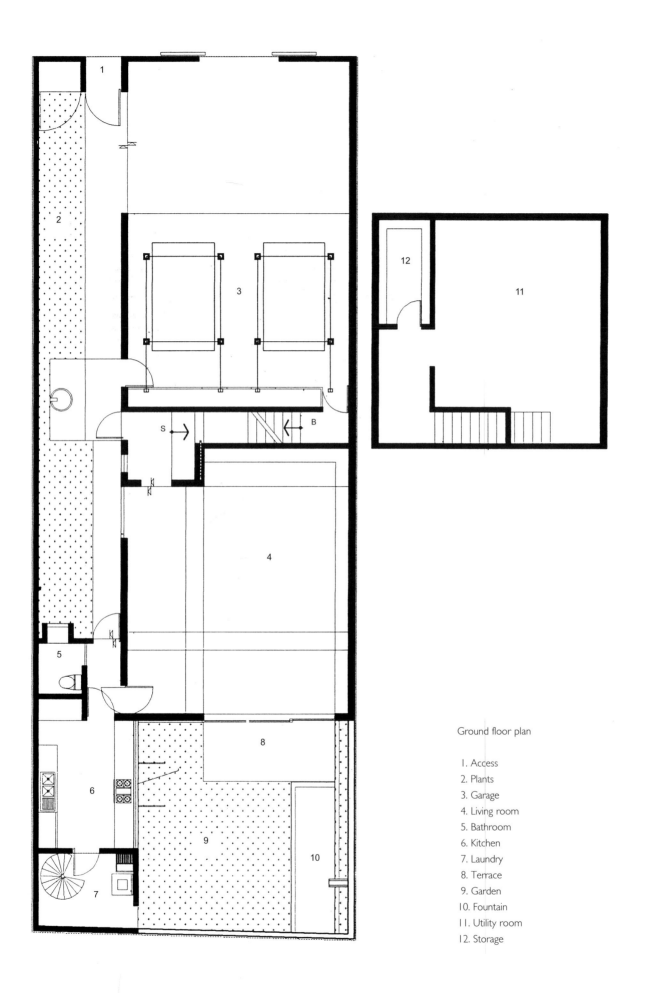

Ground floor plan

1. Access
2. Plants
3. Garage
4. Living room
5. Bathroom
6. Kitchen
7. Laundry
8. Terrace
9. Garden
10. Fountain
11. Utility room
12. Storage

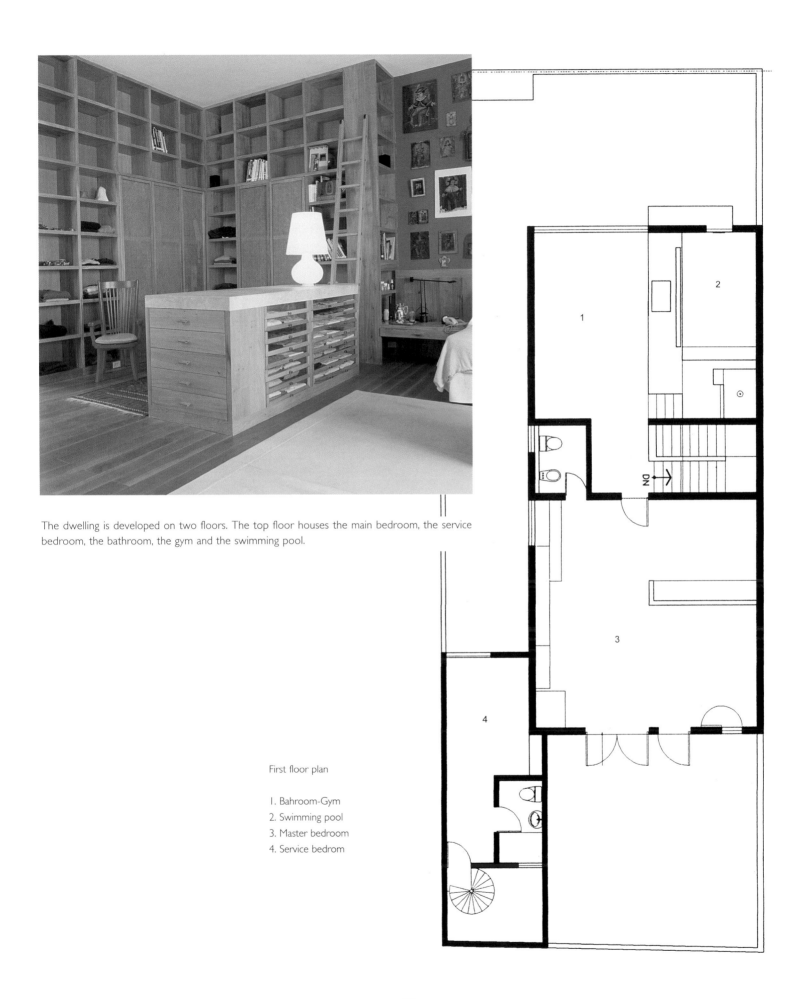

The dwelling is developed on two floors. The top floor houses the main bedroom, the service bedroom, the bathroom, the gym and the swimming pool.

First floor plan

1. Bahroom-Gym
2. Swimming pool
3. Master bedroom
4. Service bedrom

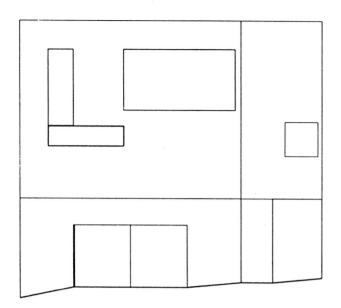

Monte Tauro St. Elevation

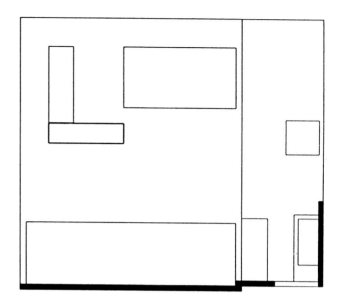

Interior elevation

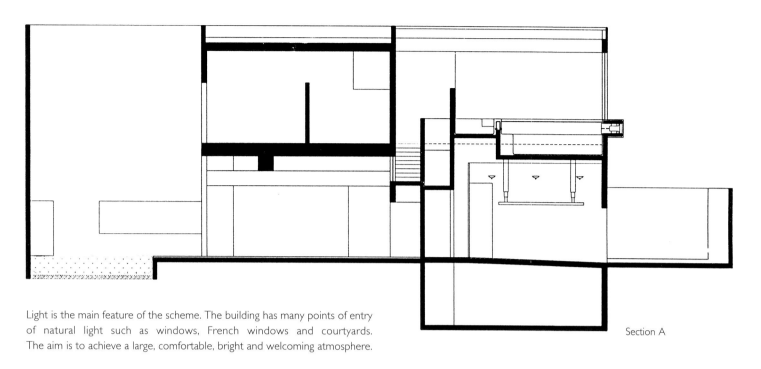

Light is the main feature of the scheme. The building has many points of entry of natural light such as windows, French windows and courtyards. The aim is to achieve a large, comfortable, bright and welcoming atmosphere.

Section A

MVRDV
Borneo Houses

Amsterdam, The Netherlands

In Borneo (Sporenburg) two dwellings stand out because of their resolution and the great spatial possibilities applied within their limited size.

The first of the dwellings, located on plot 18, is 4.2 meters wide and 16 meters high and has a spacious double-height terrace on the sea-side of the building. Initially the regulations only allowed for the construction of three floors: a high floor at street level and two more above it. Despite this, the architects were able to create four floors by building in blocks and setting one of the four levels at the rear. A long traverse section was also designed with two "closed" elements: a space with direct access to the street that serves as a garage, and another block suspended over the terrace and the water on the second level that stands out from the rest of the building and houses the bedroom and a bathroom. The remaining irregular space of the house —the kitchen-dining room, living room and study— are linked so as to provide a fluid and simple transition from one room to the next. The rooms were designed with different heights and degrees of privacy. Each one is directly connected to the exterior through an exclusive access, with the double height terrace, an overhanging window and a roof garden aligned on the rear facade.

On plot 12 a very unusual private dwelling was designed in an experiment to adapt the distribution to the narrow site. Due to this restriction and to the fact that only half of the width was used, the result is an alley and the narrowest house imaginable —only 2.5 meters wide. Breaking with normal practice, the whole length and height of the half that was built along the back street has a glass facade, while the facades facing the street and the channel were left entirely closed. This open facade rotates the house to face the alley, so that the exterior and interior are presented as a single space.

The alley accommodates three differentiated elements: a block that serves for storage whose roof slopes towards the street, providing a parking space, and two closed volumes, a block containing a guest room and bathroom, and a block that provides additional width to the studios on the first and second floor. These last two volumes are suspended in the glass facade, containing the exterior space and giving life to the alley. An extremely narrow house thus became a sufficiently spacious dwelling.

Photographs: Nicholas Kane

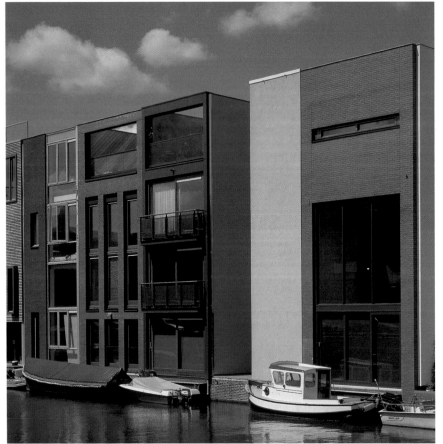

Plot 18

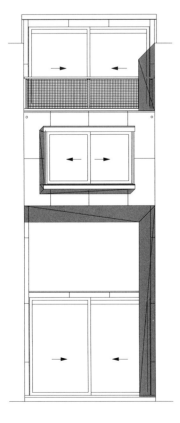

Elevation waterside

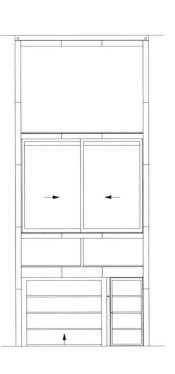

Elevation streetside

79

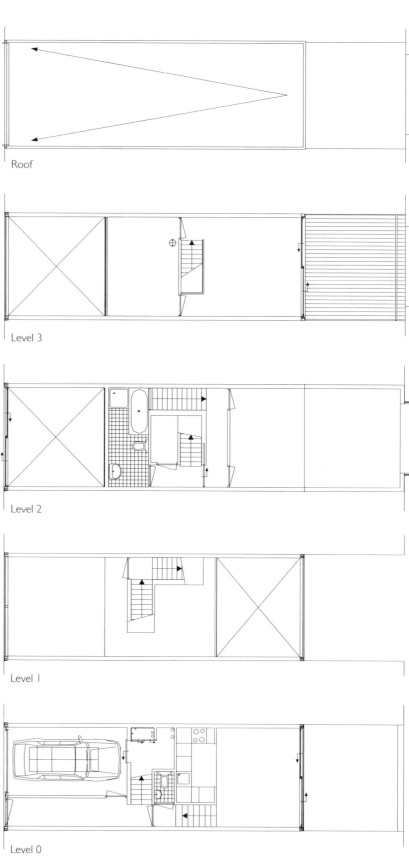

Roof

Level 3

Level 2

Level 1

Level 0

Plot 12

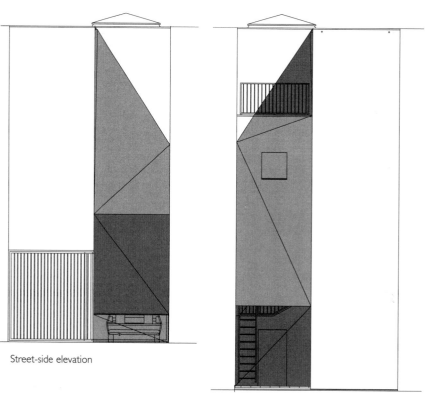

Street-side elevation

Water-side elevation

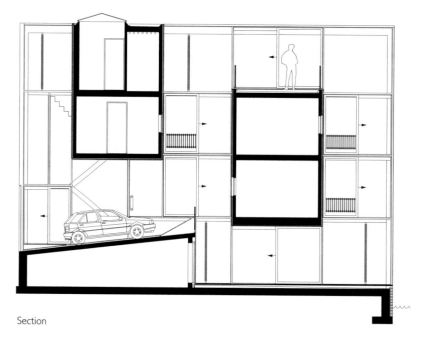

Section

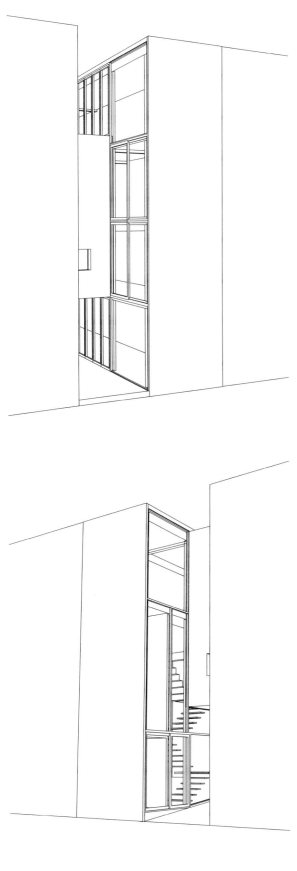

83

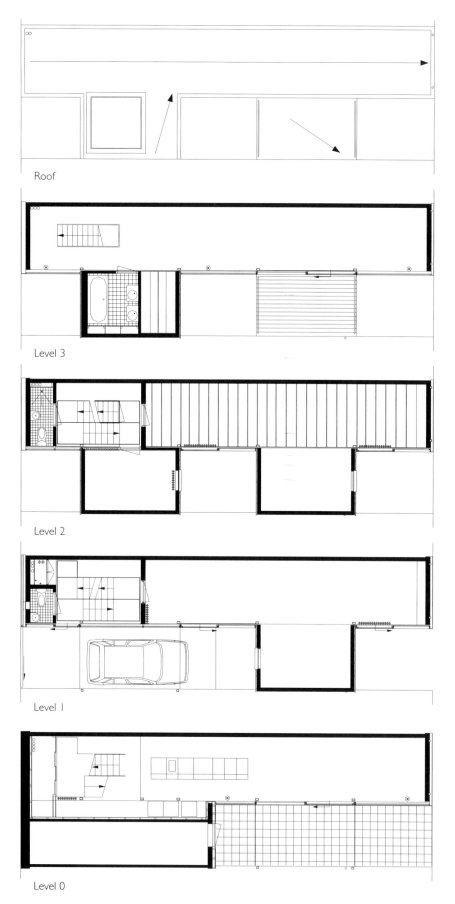

Roof

Level 3

Level 2

Level 1

Level 0

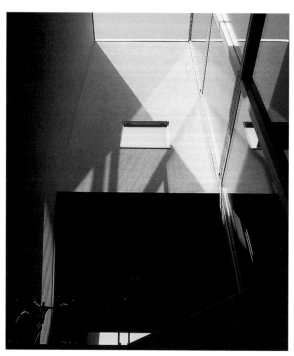

Unlike the neighboring dwellings, because the site was so narrow this house has its fully glazed main facade at the side facing the alley. Modules were added to enlarge the building and give it personality.

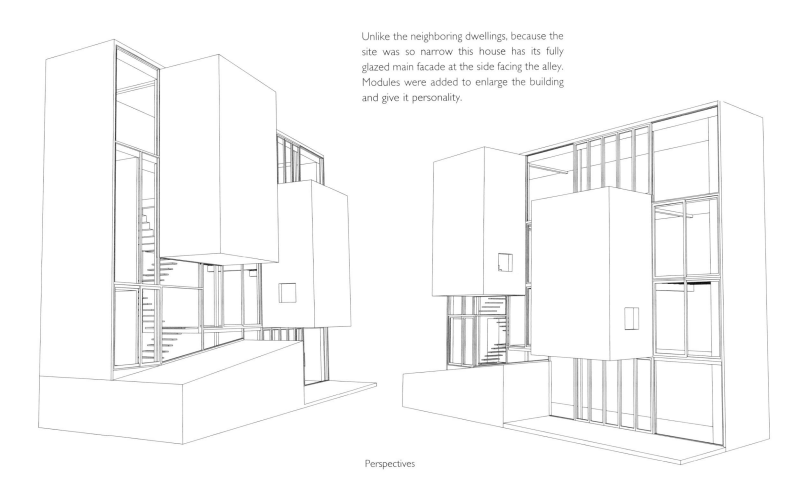

Perspectives

Alvaro Siza
Figueiredo House

Valbom-Gondomar, Portugal

Figueiredo House, in Valbom-Gondomar, is an excellent example of Alvaro Siza's mastery in composing volumes and geome-
tries of great simplicity. The architect's skill lies in the way that
he fits them together, creating new forms and physical relations
that enhance the quality of the interior spaces and the development of the visual perspectives of the exterior.

This dwelling is located on a small level plot on one side of the valley where the River Douro crosses and reaches the city of
Oporto. It is arranged on two levels in a symmetric composition
based on the intersection of two simple figures: a rectangle, where
the greater part of the layout is developed, and an octagon, which
establishes a basic structural difference between the two floors.

The ground floor is ordered by the axis of the corridor, around
which various rooms are distributed. Here, the upper level
octagon can only be discerned by the support columns.
The building extends in the form of a ship's prow, opened to
the landscape through ample windows.

The octagon plays a dominant role on the upper level. The
bedrooms gravitate toward it and the volumetric imbalance
that it creates between the levels allowed for a terrace facing
the gentle landscape of the valley.

The difference in volumes is also reflected in the facades in the
complimentary contrast between the curvature on the lower
level and the more severe geometry of the upper level.
Nevertheless, the uniform white and the modulation of openings
unify the building. Finally, a porch extends from the body of the
annex to the entrance of the house.

Photographs: Juan Rodríguez.

North-West elevation

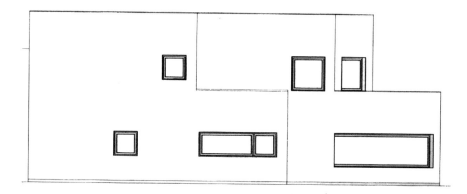

86

South East elevation

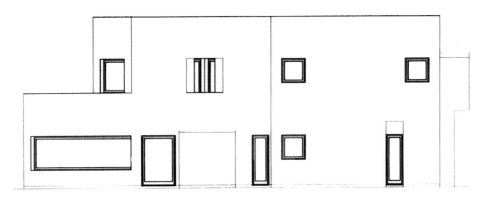

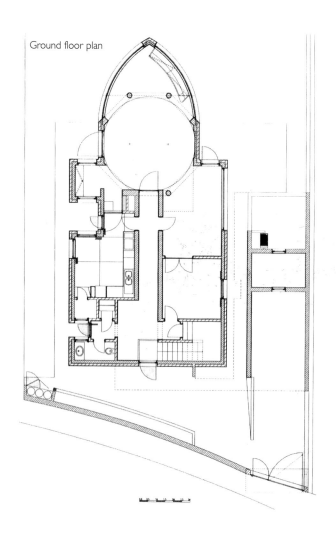

Ground floor plan

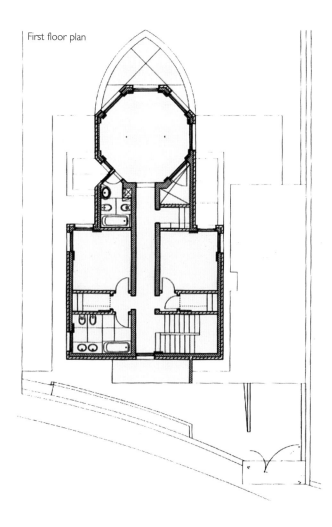

First floor plan

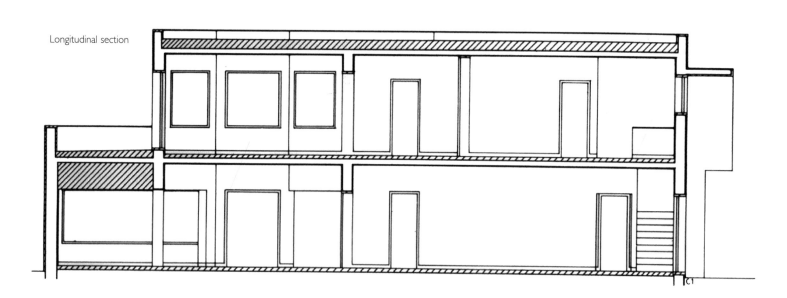

Longitudinal section

LOG ID

Residential Building in the Black Forest

Schramberg, Germany

This home for a family of four is situated on a sloping plot, close to a preexisting detached house in Schramberg, in the Black Forest, overlooking the town and the castle. The aim of the architects was to build a solar house, including a separate apartment, which would complement the neighboring house.

Access from the street above is over a footbridge in metal grating alongside the parking platform, which juts out over the garden.

Solar architecture was a basic premise of the new building from the design stage, and is clearly discernible in the ground plan. The body of the construction, with outer walls in Poroton 36.5 cm thick, is compact in order to minimize its surface area and the resulting diffusion of heat.

Solar energy is collected passively in the 64-square-meter glasshouse, which faces southwest and is shaped to take full advantage of the sun as it crosses the sky. The heat thus generated is then used actively, being distributed throughout the 360 m² of living space. The plants in the glasshouse also contribute to the health of the family by producing oxygen and bonding harmful substances.

Daylight enters through the glasshouse and also through a fanlight in the main body of the house. Beneath the fanlight, a glass reticular arrangement allows natural light to penetrate as far as the living room.

The glasshouse has a steel structure with thermal glass surfaces, while the interiors are in white mineral plaster for the walls and white marble for the floors.

The project is a successful example of how to combine environmentalism and high-quality detached housing.

Photographs: Reiner Blunck

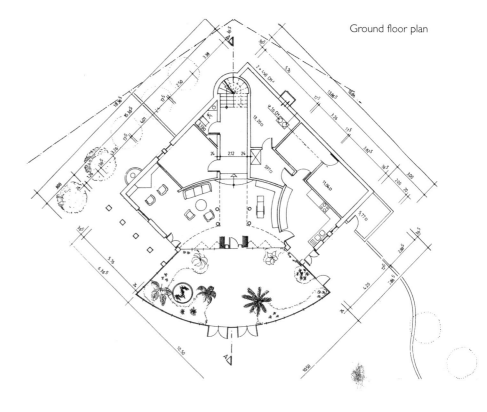

Ground floor plan

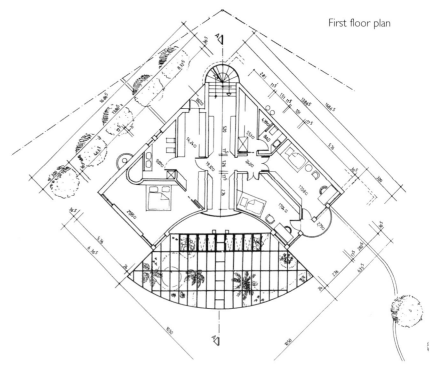

First floor plan

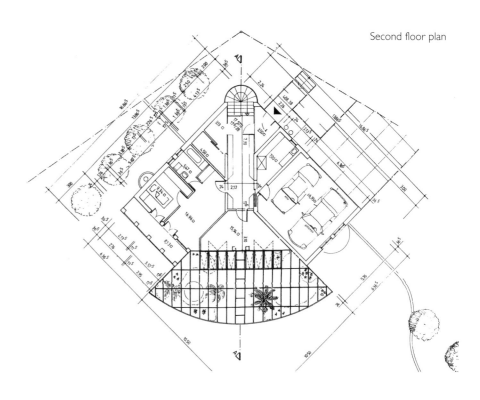

Second floor plan

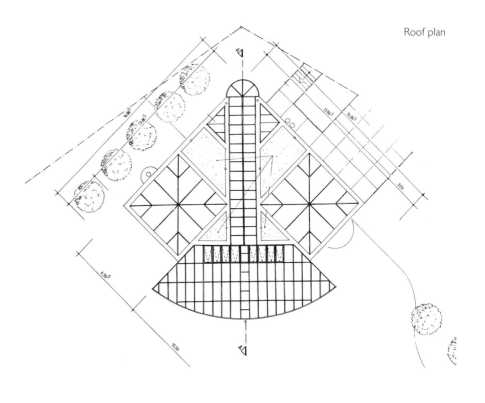

Roof plan

North elevation

South elevation

Koh Kitayama
Omni Quarter

Tokyo, Japan

This multi-purpose building, which is located in one of Tokyo's most sophisticated areas, has a basement floor, which houses an atelier, and four stories, covering a total floor area of 863m². Living quarters are on the third and fourth floors; a shop occupies the first and second floors. A spacious, atrium-like space has been annexed onto the south side. This space serves the dual purpose of providing a stairwell which does not obstruct the central living space and an air layer that is part of a double-skin environmental control device.

This latter function is part of the architects' philosophy of designing structures which handle environmental conditions in a more rational manner: it is the inhabitants who decide when their home needs a "change of clothes", opening and closing household fixtures in response to the given climate and season.

This building also displays a characteristic which is not only typical of this studio's work, but to Asian house architecture in general: a planar format, with hallways and stairways placed at the periphery of the living area, thereby creating spaces which are easily adaptable to changes in daily living.

The building is an equal span rigid-frame structure with support columns on the inside, which frees up space in the hallways.

Photographs: Nobuaki Nakagawa

Site plan

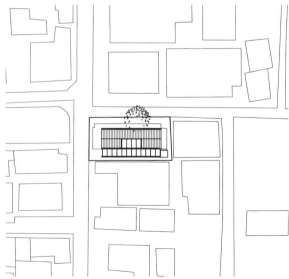

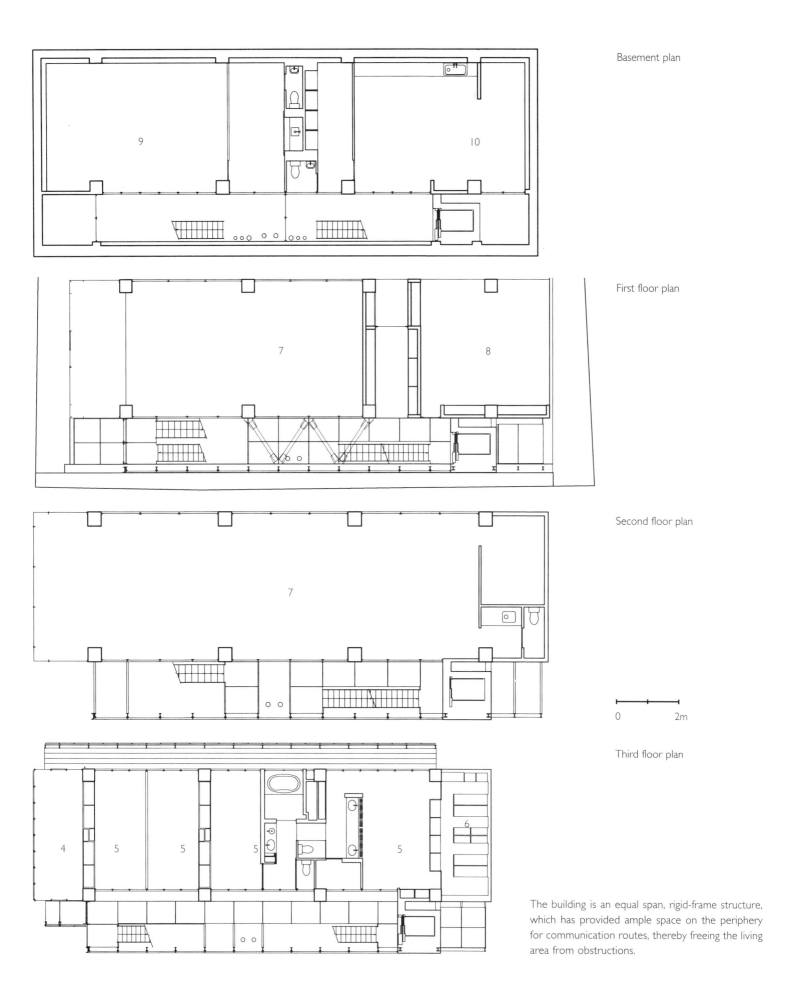

Basement plan

First floor plan

Second floor plan

0   2m

Third floor plan

The building is an equal span, rigid-frame structure, which has provided ample space on the periphery for communication routes, thereby freeing the living area from obstructions.

Fourth floor plan

1. Work space
2. Pantry
3. Multi-use room
4. Atelier
5. Private room
6. Cloak
7. Tenant
8. Parking area
9. Gallery
10. Ceramics atelier

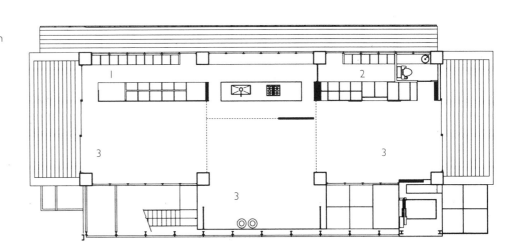

Feeling that Japanese architecture has tended in the past several years toward sterile and homogenous spaces, this studio sought a more "user-friendly" design. All skylights and openings can be opened or closed according to the season or weather conditions.

Rick Joy
Convent Avenue Studios

Tucson, USA

For this project comprising three new houses and a restored casita, Rick Joy designed buildings "of their own time" whilst respecting the historic setting of a desert climate and using simple building materials.

He laid a new stone foundation for the house, resurfaced its adobe walls with lime plaster and added new mechanical services as well as a new bathroom and kitchen. The former entrances to the two old row houses now serve as gateways to the project's front courtyard.

All new elements are clearly identified by either color or material. For example, new concrete-block walls running through the site are plastered, then painted lime green, while restored adobe walls are kept white. Joy designed the three new live-work studios as rammed-earth structures as a way of emulating the simplicity of adobe using an alternative building system.

Made of dirt mixed with a small amount of Portland cement that is compacted inside metal forms, these structures are thick-walled buildings that require no reinforcing and no internal or external finishes.

Starting with simple shed forms that could fit like jigsaw pieces on a small parcel of land, Joy developed a wedge-shaped plan for the houses. The wedge also opened up outdoor spaces between units that could be used as private courtyards.

Although building codes allowed the architect to place the houses along one property line, Joy set them back to allow north and south-facing windows and to create the courtyards. Creosote bushes salvaged from other sites are planted throughout the project, while old corrugated metal is used for a perimeter fence. Dirt, gravel and old stones are the main paving materials.

Inside the houses, the thick walls are the dominant feature, complemented by rough-sawn Douglas-fir roof beams, concrete floors and fir ceilings and windows.

Sunlight is treated as a precious commodity, being almost totally blocked on the east and west, and brought in through a narrow skylight above the bedroom and through windows that frame tight views of the courtyards.

Photographs: Rick Joy

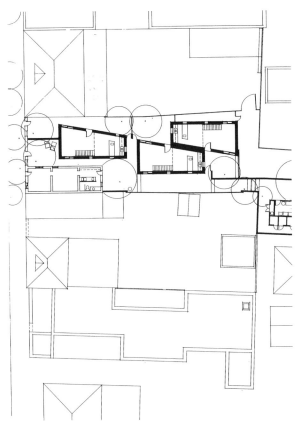

General floor plan

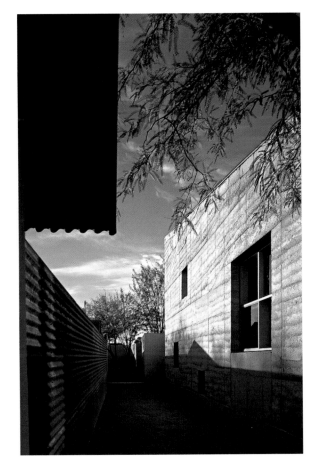

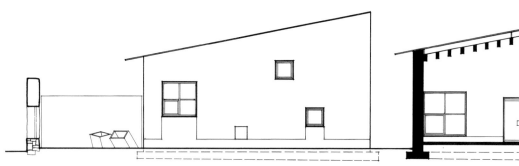

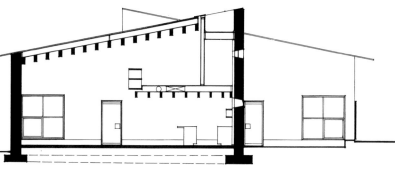

Longitudinal section

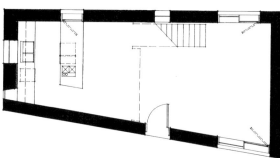

Standard plans of the apartments

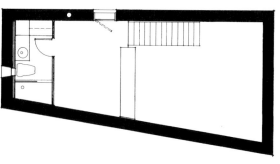

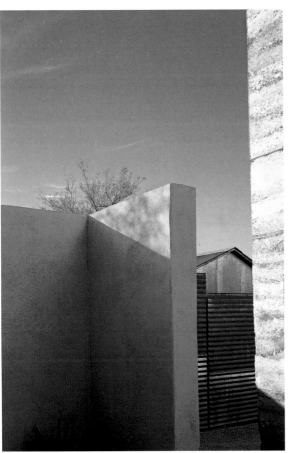

The interior of the dwelling was organized so as to leave a wide and well-lit space for the study area.

Peter W. Schmidt
Studio House in Pforzheim

Pforzheim, Germany

The classical building assignment —house combined with studio— along with the considerations of site and program is also a typological challenge in dealing with principle solutions. The two architectural bodies, house and studio, are inserted into the topography of the landscape in such a way that a clear functional separation is apparent. Simultaneously through the positioning of the buildings a symbiosis is achieved, giving the exterior space and its transition a domestic character. Both buildings face their own individual courts at the site boundaries, which enable access to the buildings.

The studio has a very clear modular system that is followed through to the structure of the interior architecture. In opposition to the studio, the arrangement of windows and facade openings of the house has a compositional structure. The body of the house, measuring 15x13x9 m, is reduced in the top two levels, where two private spaces have terraces. The different treatment of the two facades has the result that the overlapping surfaces become an "interior facade" with deep incisions, while the openings of the exterior facades are shallower and bound to the facade surface.

The different architectonic formulation of the two buildings follow the same design principles in their use of materials as well as in their details. Construction and detail are arranged within the concept and support the architectural expression.

Photographs: Stefan Müller

East elevation

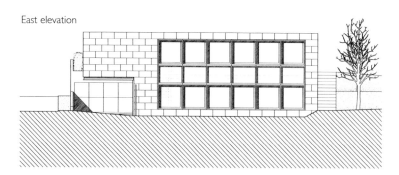

Section AA

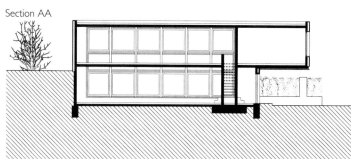

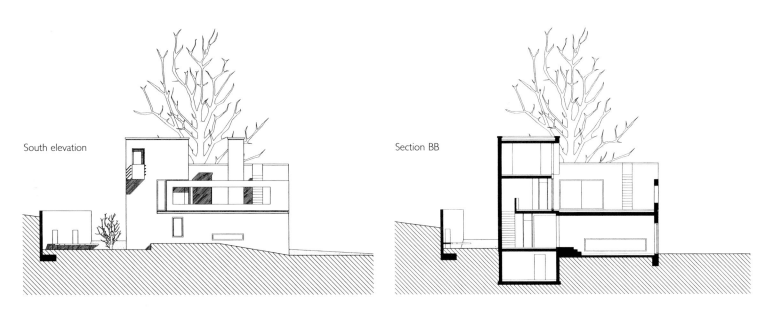

South elevation

Section BB

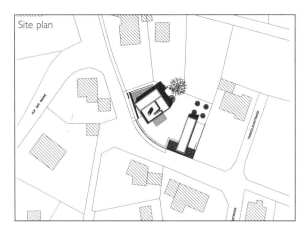

Site plan

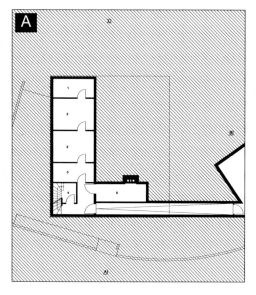

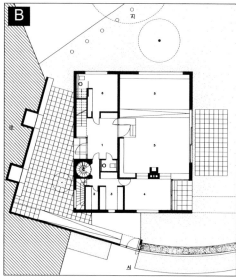

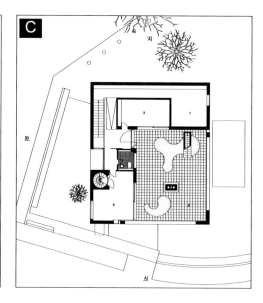

A Basement floor plan
1. Wine cellar
2. Cellar
3. Wash room
4. Technical installations
5. Heating

B Ground floor plan
1. Entrance atrium
2. Wardrobe
3. Kitchen
4. Dining room
5. Living room
6. Guest room

C First floor plan
1. Library
2. Children's room
3. Terrace

D Second floor plan
1. Bedroom
2. Dressing room
3. Terrace

E Studio ground floor plan
1. Atelier
2. Archives
3. Garage

F Studio upper floor plan
1. Atelier
2. Meeting room

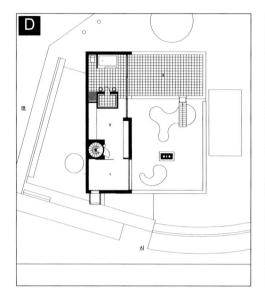

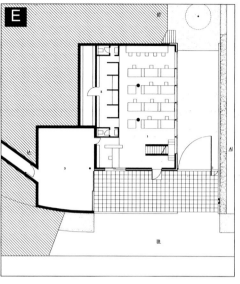

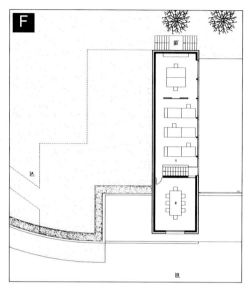

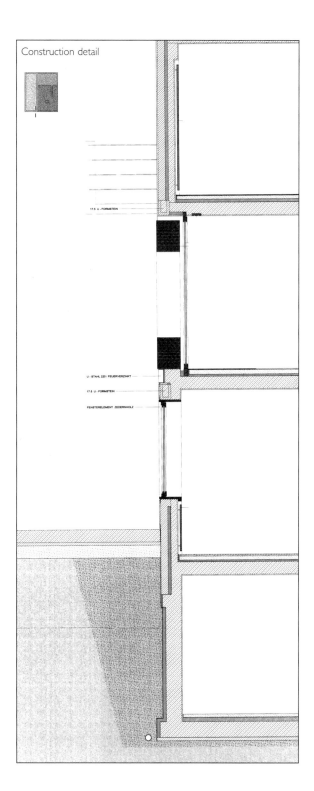

Construction detail

17.5 U - FORMSTEIN

U - STAHL 220 / FEUERVERZINKT

17.5 U - FORMSTEIN

FENSTERELEMENT ZEDERNHOLZ

Cheng Design
Hogan/Mayo Residence

Rancho Santa Fe, California, USA

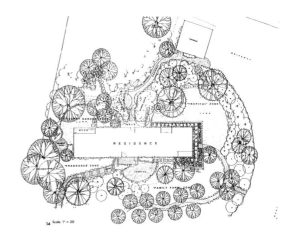

At the time of its acquisition, the site on which this dwelling stands was occupied by an old ranch. The clients decided to demolish it and build a new house combining clarity and warmth. A long rectangular ground plan similar to that of the original construction was chosen. The main entrance, the private entrance, the ground floor rooms and the main bedroom converge in an interior-exterior space that acts as a sheltered area and a pergola. The two entrances seek to produce the sensation of transit: a stone walkway forms the private rear entrance, while the main entrance is formed by a staircase similar to that of a ship, with steel cable handrails.

The construction is clad in corrugated metal sheet, which was also used on the roof to optimise rainwater drainage. The discreet presence of wooden strips and boarding on the exterior evokes the vernacular constructions of the area. The walls of the main bedroom, the ground floor corridor and the kitchen were built with reinforced concrete cast in situ.

The walkway of the rear entrance ends in a concrete block stamped with symbols from the I Ching. The two hexagrams on the wall represent the concepts "reduction" and "limitation", interpretations taken from the divinatory methods of The Book of Changes. As in all Cheng Design projects, the clients, the manufacturer, the site foreman and Fu-Tu Cheng, director of the Cheng design study, threw their coins into the air just before laying the foundations of the house in order to establish a connection with the spirit of change and non-permanence and to obtain spiritual guidance for the participants in the project. In the house we can also find other symbols that represent "water", "infinity" and "work", as well as several objects that were recovered from the site or -like the doorknob- found in the local flea-market.

Photographs: Debbie Beacham

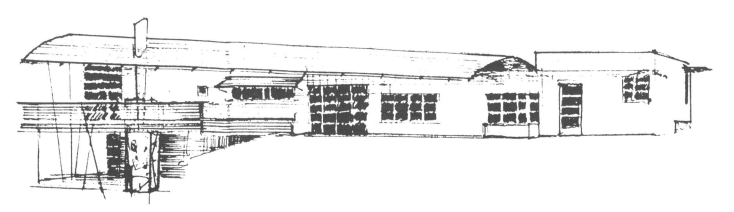

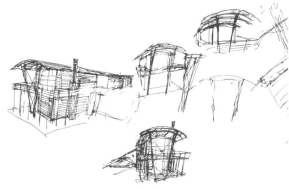

The house's exterior cladding combines wood, glass and corrugated metal. The latter is shown here to be a highly versatile material, which combines a light look with structural durability.

Upper floor plan

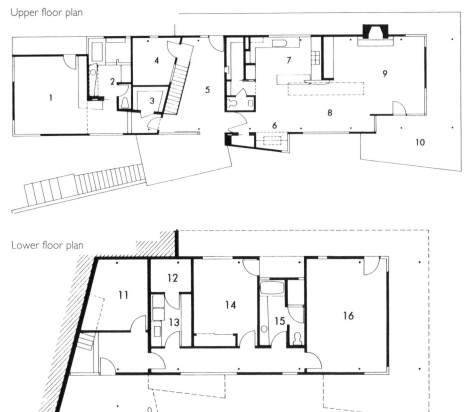

Lower floor plan

1. Master Bedroom
2. Master Bathroom
3. Closet
4. Office
5. Dog trot
6. Main Entry
7. Kitchen
8. Dining Room
9. Living Room
10. Deck
11. Storage
12. Mechanical Room
13. Laundry
14. Bedroom
15. Bathroom
16. Library

Large picture windows maximize the light and elongated skylights running the length of the corridor usher in light from above. The industrial look of the exterior of the home is reflected in the interior with steel and wire handrails, bare structures and juxtapositions of levels.

GAD architecture
A House with Three Eras

Istanbul, Turkey

The brief called for the rehabilitation of a four-story house in Istanbul with three clearly identifiable "eras". The facades each belong to different periods, with approximately fifty years separating each. The floor plan was slender and long with a spacious garden enveloping the house, which faces the Bosporus Strait and is soaked in natural daylight on the south-facing side.

One long side facade and the facade facing the sea were renovated by the building's second owner according to the prevailing architectural standards and approaches of the day. In this latest phase of renovation, the program was especially respectful in its treatment of the facade bearing traces of the rationalist period, as well as the facade with the charming bay windows.

Much of the material used in the renovation process was recycled from the original building.

The newly-renovated house has been arranged according to the owners' wish to have plenty of space and privacy for overnight guests. Each floor functions separately from the others, so that guests and inhabitants can move about freely without disturbing each other.

The lush garden, created over a hundred years ago, is a remnant of the original owner's preference for the outdoors and now rises to the height of the house's top level. It is laid out on four levels, the bottom levels of which provide the home with vegetables and fruit on a daily basis.

Photographs: Yavuz Draman

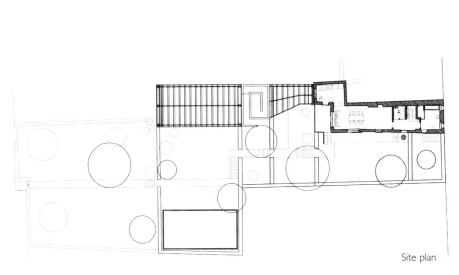

Site plan

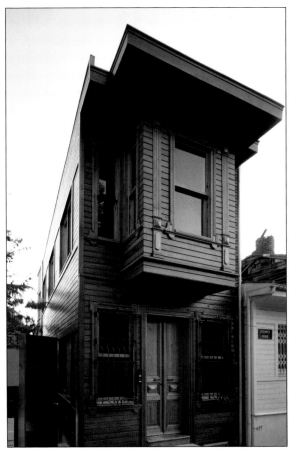

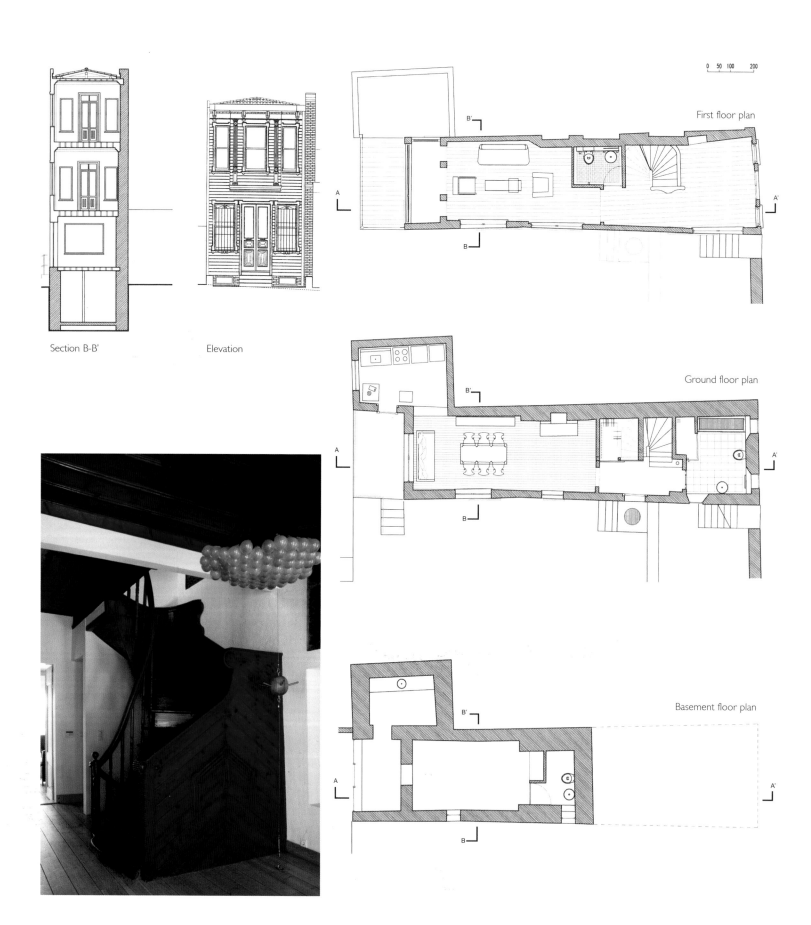

Section B-B'

Elevation

First floor plan

0 50 100   200

Ground floor plan

Basement floor plan

124

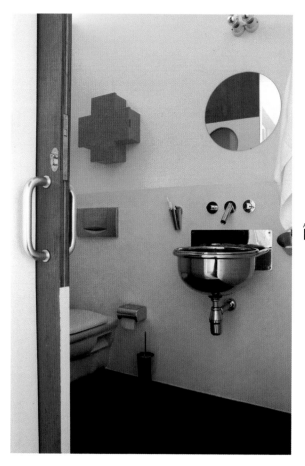

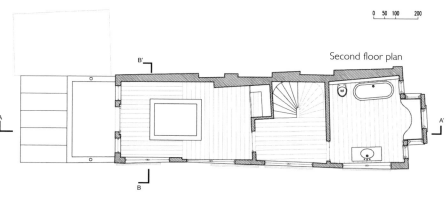

Second floor plan

0 50 100   200

John Pawson
Audi Apartment

Amsterdam, The Netherlands

The architect John Pawson is the author of this calm and minimal dwelling inside an eighteenth-century building beside a canal in the city of Amsterdam.

In keeping with the attitude of this British architect's work, the approach to the old spaces of this dwelling-studio was quiet and moderate, careful and essential. The client, Pierre Audi, the director of the Amsterdam Opera, already knew the architect. In fact, years before, he had commissioned Pawson to design his dwelling in London, when he was working as a theater director in the city. For his Dutch apartment, Audi asked Pawson for a fluid and coherent interior with the architectural quality of the historical building, and interior planning endowed with a certain spatial order.

The functional layout of the building, on six levels, is structured as follows: dining room and kitchen in the basement, study-library on the ground floor and living area, the guest bedrooms with their respective toilets and the main bedroom distributed on the first, second, third and fourth floors. The basement is where Pawson found the largest number of original elements to conserve in his design. A large original chimney presides over the dining room area, and the kitchen, which is joined with the dining room, features the old exhaust hood and the original tiles on the walls.

The access level is a more "public" area, in which a large study area and a small library are created. On the top floor, the main bedroom is one of the most outstanding spaces, typical of the buildings in this area of the city and featuring the large exposed wooden beams of the pitched roof.

Photographs: Christopher Kircherer

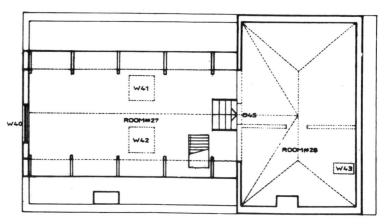

Fourth floor plan

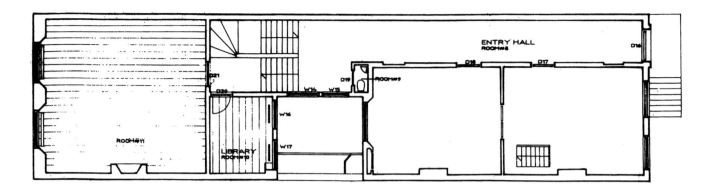

Ground floor plan

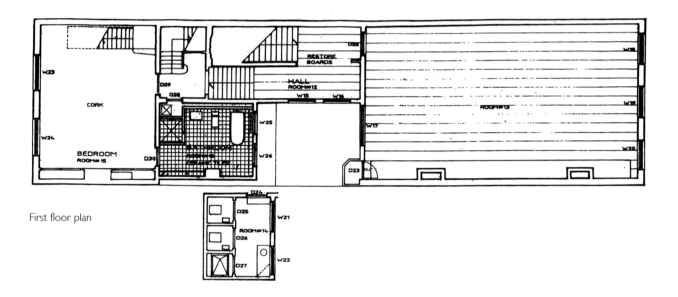

First floor plan

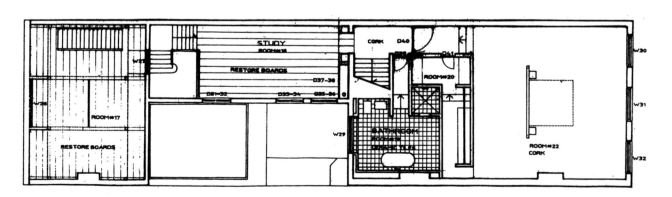

Second floor plan

Engelen Moore
House in Redfern

Sydney, Australia

This two-story house has been built on a vacant plot of land formerly occupied by two terrace houses, in a street otherwise composed of houses, warehouses and apartments of varying ages and sizes. The local council insisted that it read as two terrace-type houses rather than as a warehouse. The front elevation is divided into two vertical bays. The major horizontal elements are aligned with the adjoining terraced houses, and each bay relates to these houses proportionally. The internal planning reflects this two-bay arrangement at the front, while the rear elevation expresses the full 6m high, 7m wide internal volume. There was a very limited budget for this project, so a simple strategy was developed to construct a low-cost shell composed of a steel portal framed structure with concrete block external skins on the long sides, lined internally with plasterboard. The front and rear parapets and blade walls are clad with compressed fiber cement sheets. This shell is painted white throughout. Within this white shell are placed a series of more refined and rigorously detailed elements differentiated by their aluminum or grey paint finish.

The front elevation is made up of six vertical panels, the lower level being clad in Alucobond aluminum composite sheet, the left hand panel being the 3.3m high front door, and the three panels on the right hand side forming the garage door. The upper level is made up of operable extruded aluminum louvers, enabling it to be adjusted from transparency to opacity.

The 6m high west-facing glass wall is made up of six individual panels, which slide and stack to one side, allowing the entire rear elevation to be opened up. This not only spatially extends the interior into the courtyard, but also, in combination with the louvered front elevation, allows exceptional control of cross ventilation to cool the house in summer, while allowing very good solar penetration to warm the house in winter. In summer, this western glass wall is screened from the sun by a large eucalyptus tree on the adjoining property.

Photographs: Ross Honeysett

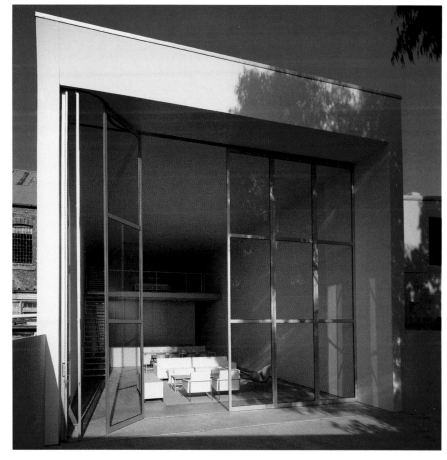

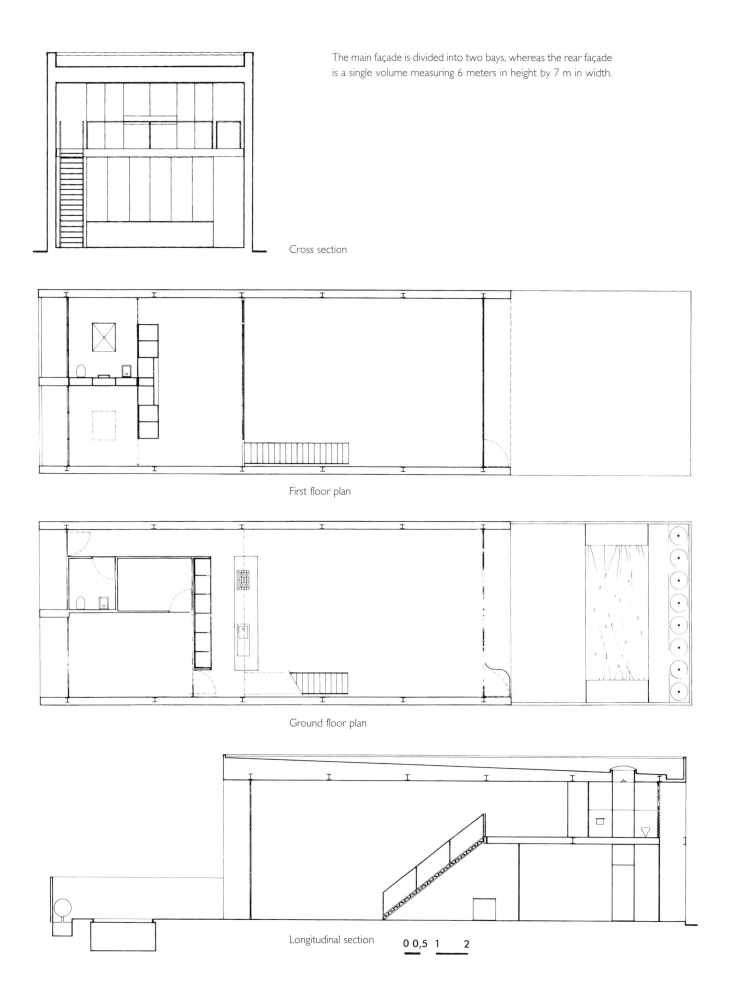

The main façade is divided into two bays, whereas the rear façade is a single volume measuring 6 meters in height by 7 m in width.

Cross section

First floor plan

Ground floor plan

Longitudinal section

0 0,5 1   2

The rooms of the upper floor are fitted with mobile aluminum shutters that can be adjusted to allow for complete transparency or opacity.

The furniture was designed by the architects. The basic requirements were that they should be inexpensive and lightweight for easy mobility.

Mutsue Hayakusa
(Cell Space Architects)
House in Motoazabu

Tokyo, Japan

Designed for a couple in their fifties, this small residence consists of three floors joined by a spiral staircase. Because the site is small with an unusual shape, the design team has explored new options by using alternate angles and contrast.

The two garages are separated from the entrance by curved glass, which gives an expanded reflection and creates the illusion of space so necessary on this restricted site. The white floor of the garages is used to reflect natural light into the home. The clients' car is reflected by the mirror onto the entrance ceiling, thereby enhancing the feeling of spaciousness. As the home has been designed for an elderly couple one of the important considerations was that it should allow for easy wheelchair access. The home has an elevator located near the entrance.

In the bedroom, soft natural light from the balcony is filtered through louvers. The space is flexible and can be adjusted to suit varying needs and preferences.

Carved movable partitions clad in silver Japanese paper can be moved to divide the room. A closet mirror visually broadens the space.

The entire living space is ensconced in softly pleated wooden walls and ceilings.

The hard image of the exterior view is broken on the third floor by willow louvers. The window reflects the pleated wooden wall at night and visually extends the space.

The kitchen and dining room comprise a single, brightly-lit space.

Photographs: Satoshi Asakawa / Katsuhisa Kida

Site plan

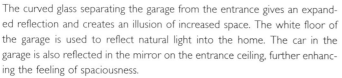

The curved glass separating the garage from the entrance gives an expanded reflection and creates an illusion of increased space. The white floor of the garage is used to reflect natural light into the home. The car in the garage is also reflected in the mirror on the entrance ceiling, further enhancing the feeling of spaciousness.

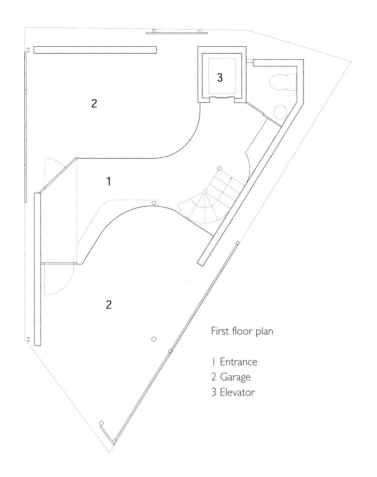

First floor plan

1 Entrance
2 Garage
3 Elevator

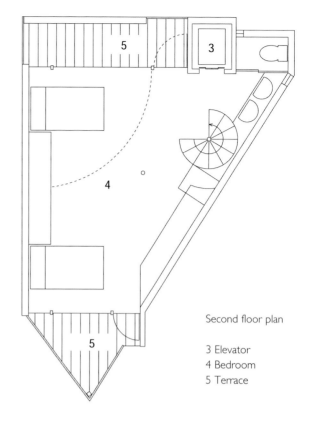

Second floor plan

3 Elevator
4 Bedroom
5 Terrace

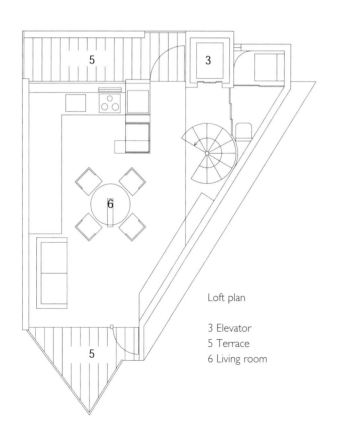

Loft plan

3 Elevator
5 Terrace
6 Living room

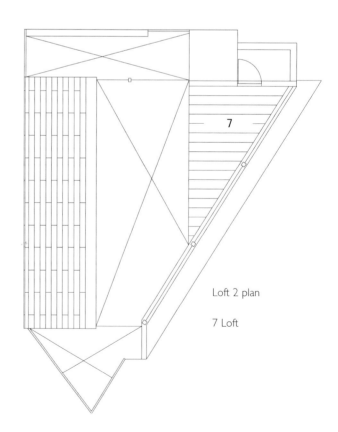

Loft 2 plan

7 Loft

ROOM

142

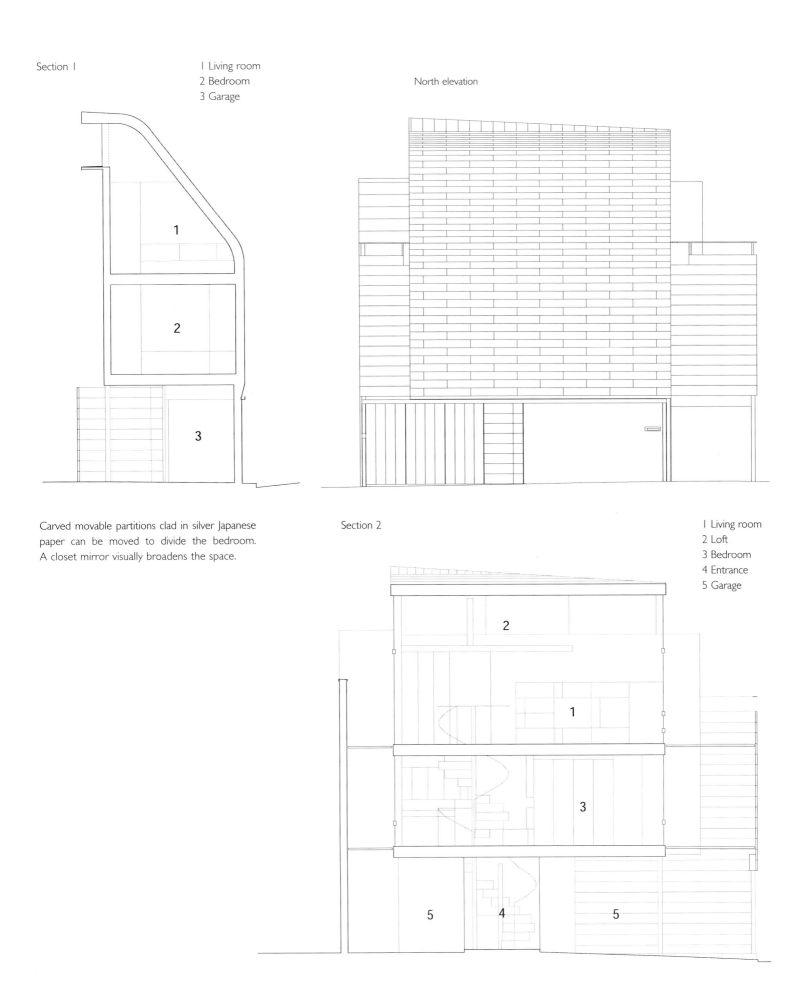

Section 1

1 Living room
2 Bedroom
3 Garage

North elevation

Carved movable partitions clad in silver Japanese paper can be moved to divide the bedroom. A closet mirror visually broadens the space.

Section 2

1 Living room
2 Loft
3 Bedroom
4 Entrance
5 Garage

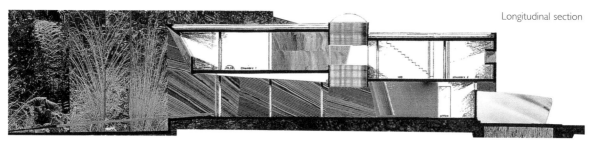

Longitudinal section

Christophe Lab
Film House

Paris, France

This very long and narrow plot of land (approximately 35x4.5 m), crossing the block from street to street and walled in on both sides, constituted a serious challenge to the architect in designing a home with sufficient light and space in which to live comfortably. The client's occupation —closely tied to the film industry— provided the inspiration behind the design scheme, with framed views and sequential spaces.

The concrete facade of this home —whose floor plan takes on the form of a strip of film— has been conceived as a camera obscura, with a giant lens drawing light into the second floor and, below that, sliding glass doors providing access. Yet, this "camera house" is also a "screen house" — a projection inside the camera itself.

As side views along the length of the construction were impossible, an alternative for bringing light into the home was desperately needed. A cylindrical covered well draws natural light down into the center of the home, where light from the two end facades hardly penetrates.

The walls of this central patio have been painted a bright, cheerful yellow to provide the necessary contrast to the sober gray of the carpet and ceiling of the interior and in order to channel and reflect a warm, diffused light throughout the two floors that it passes through.

Space was reserved on both ends of the site for a garage, which has been conceived as a large toolbox, and a garden, which can be viewed as an extension of the living room in the summer months. Stairs on the second floor lead to the roof terrace above.

Photographs: Anna Khan

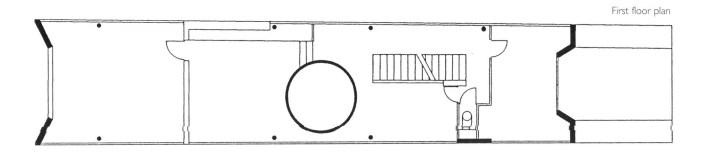

First floor plan

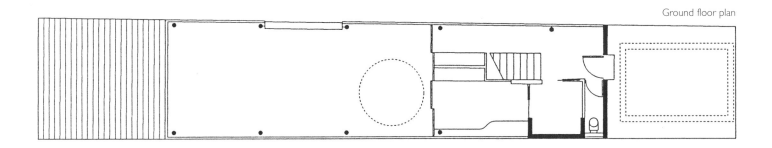

Ground floor plan

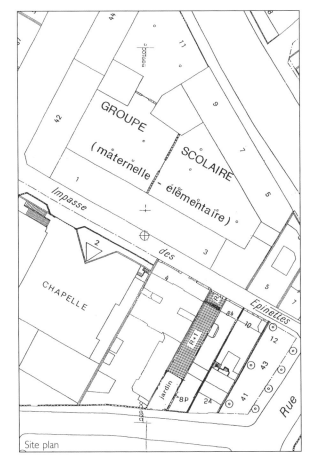

Site plan

Longitudinal section

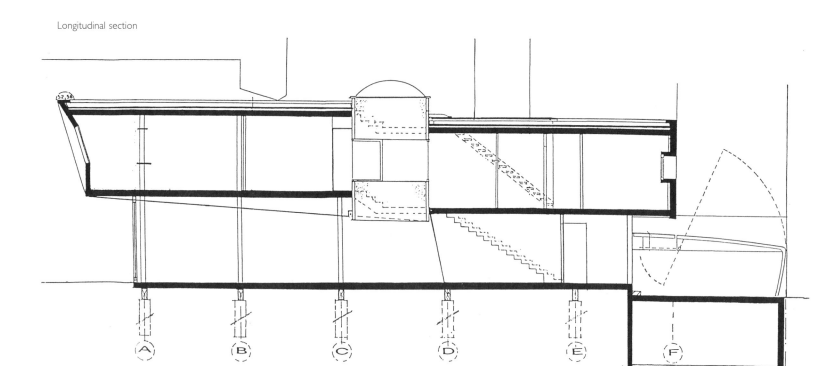

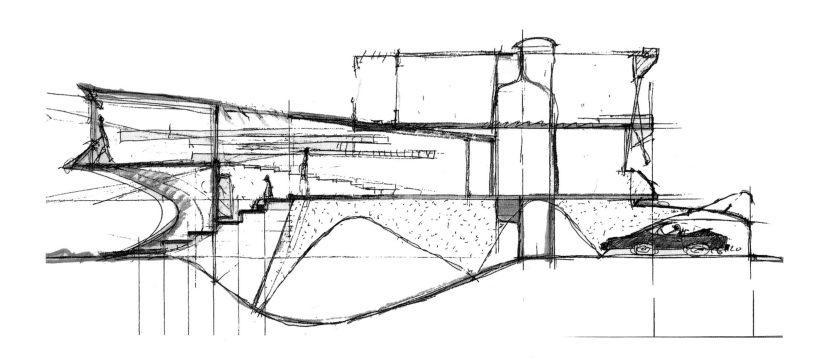

148

Koichiro Ishiguro
White Woods

Tokyo, Japan

To satisfy the clients' (a working couple with a daughter) wish to be able to spend as much time as possible together as a family, and to allow for future function changes, an integrated space with sufficient volume was the objective. The basic space structuring method consisted of a shelter of thin, rigid-frame structure ensuring the volume of 900m^3, the maximum according to this structure's regulations, into which a floor space of 200m^2 (a "stage") was inserted as a required function.

The site is located in the midst of a crowded residential area, flanked by buildings on all of its four sides. Sunlight and views of the sky are secured with an opening in the ceiling. In the center of the floor plan, a well-hole topped by a skylight amplifies the natural lighting, filling this volume of considerable depth. Stages were inserted at positions decided upon after examination of how these views and functions might relate to each other.

The composition of the house resulted in a loose division into two -bedroom and living/dining room- sections, bisected by the huge glass plate lining the well-hole.

The above-mentioned features call forth elements which involve "individual times", such as a piece of sky, family life, movements of sun and moon, and the growth of trees. A multi-layered series of platforms yields a viewpoint looking through these layers, where an act of crossing such a space involves integrating various experiences. Compared to loft apartments in Manhattan, which are typical examples of living space with a clear homogeneity, this "multi-layered loft" is as simple and calm as a forest. And yet, it offers the possibility of creating a diverse, complex space.

Photographs: K. Takada

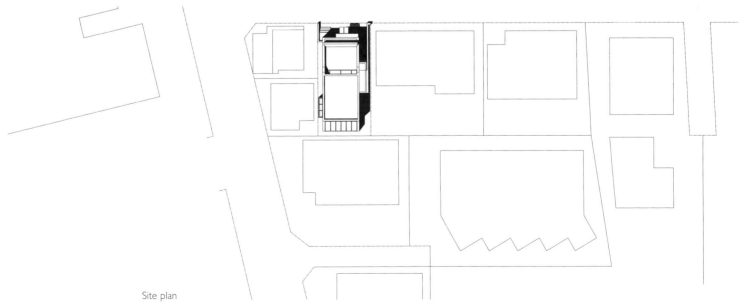

Site plan

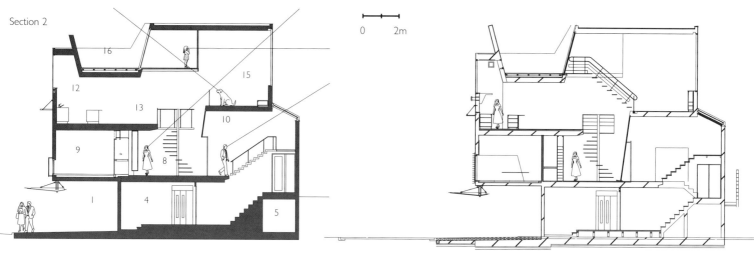

Section 2

16
15
12
13
10
9
8
1
4
5

0   2m

1. Car port
2. Bicycle parking
3. Entrance
4. Play room
5. Storeroom
6. Washroom
7. Bathroom
8. Entrance hall
9. Tatami room
10. Bedroom
11. Closet
12. Kitchen
13. Dining room
14. Laundry
15. Living room
16. Terrace

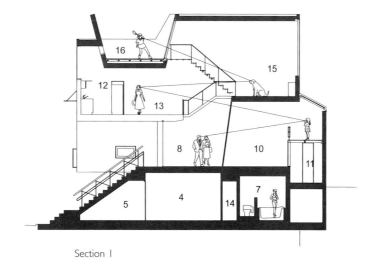

Section 1

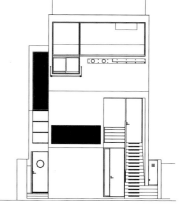

North elevation

157

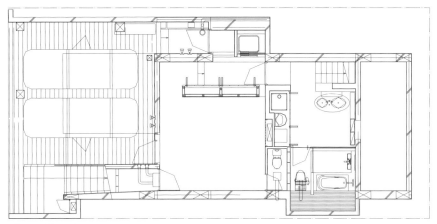

Ground floor plan

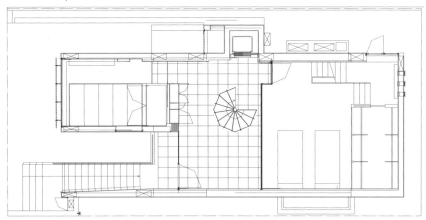

First floor plan

In the center of the floor plan, a well-hole topped by a skylight amplifies the natural light. The house is divided loosely into two sections -bedroom and living/dining room- bisected by the huge glass plate lining the well-hole.

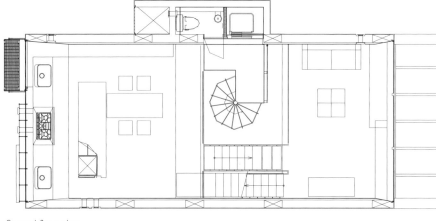

Second floor plan

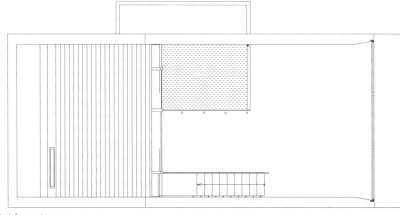

Third floor plan

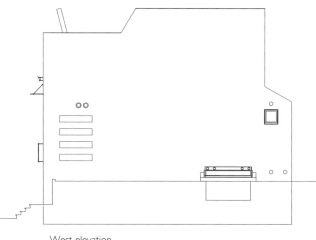

West elevation

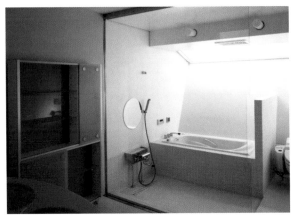

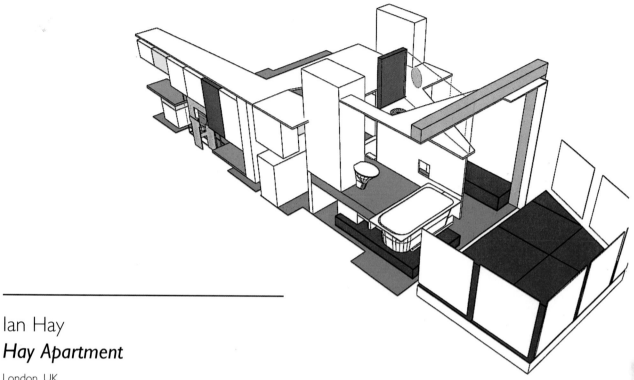

Ian Hay
Hay Apartment

London, UK

Housed in two rooms on the first floor of a modest Georgian terrace off Tottenham Court Road, and occupying only 320ft^2, this apartment was designed around the premise that Hay wanted a spacious house in a very small space. He refused to make the compromises usual in studio-sized flats, such as having a shower instead of a bath, or putting the kitchen in the living room. Instead, he began by calculating the minimum space required to cook, or for a double bed, then looked at ways in which these functions could be combined within the limited space.

The flat may have everything, but it is not always where you would expect to find it. The bathroom, for instance, is on a platform above the bed, and from the bath, there is a choice of views: you can open up a hatch to watch a small TV beside the bed, or see through the kitchen into the front room. The front room itself doubles as a work pace, with a large table that folds down from the wall so that Hay can run his practice from home. One key to the success of this very tight conversion is the play on transparency. Neither the bathroom nor the kitchen are treated as enclosed rooms, and surprising sightlines run through the flat, so that the claustrophobic feeling associated with tight, boxed-in spaces is avoided.

Photographs: Richard Glover

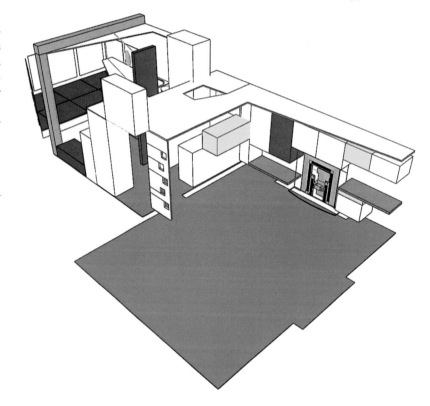

Access floor plan

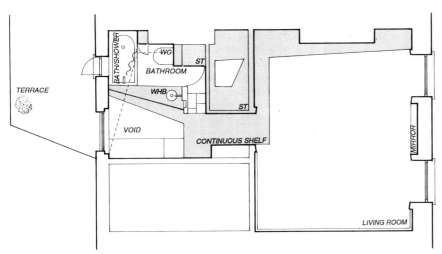

Upper floor plan

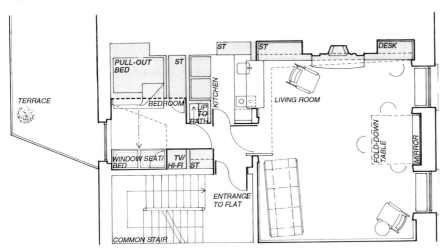

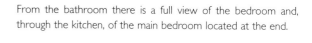

From the bathroom there is a full view of the bedroom and, through the kitchen, of the main bedroom located at the end.

TEN Arquitectos
IA House

Valle Bravo, Mexico

The architects Bernardo Gómez-Pimienta and Enrique Norten designed this dwelling, built on a hillside in the Bravo Valley overlooking a lake, with the aim of creating a space in which the beauty of the landscape was a positive feature but presented no obstacle to the distinctive character of the scheme. The site has stone walls covered with earth and gravel, and it was decided to maintain these fragments unfinished and to place a glass prism on them. The heights of these walls thus define the levels of the project. The building has a series of strips parallel to the lake and perpendicular to the slope that define the different platforms of the interior and the exterior spaces.

The glass volume of Cartesian clarity and strict order organizes the architectural program by means of its structure, because it houses the living room, dining room and master bedroom, all separated by a low volume that contains the service areas. This glass prism sits on a stone base in which two bedrooms are located. The living room window runs along the facade, opening the space toward the exterior and the lake.

The wooden ceiling is supported by thin columns, which makes it seem to float on the interior walls without touching them, thus creating spatial continuity. The sloping roof responds to the demands of the urban regulations. Its northern aspect was used to extend it toward the exterior by means of a wooden pergola, thus creating a sun filter with views of the lake. The floor is also extended toward the courtyard, and its intersection with the pergola forms the inhabited space. This solution also makes it possible to expand the internal space outwards and thus to eliminate the limit between interior and exterior.

A minimum number of materials was used for the construction of this dwelling and the colors were chosen to enhance the exterior (the lake, mountains and sky), and to emphasize the changes in the vegetation and the landscape.

Photographs: Luis Gordoa, Frank Visser

The glass volume, which is both transparent and translucent, offers a continuous view and creates a play of transparencies and opacities that varies according to the time of day, as it absorbs and reflects the colors of the exterior.

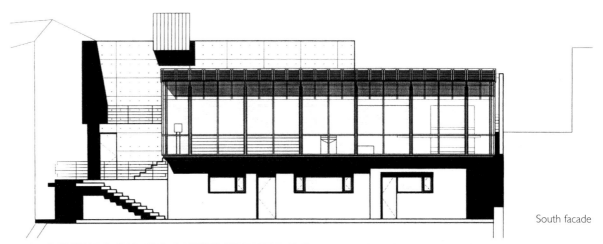

South facade

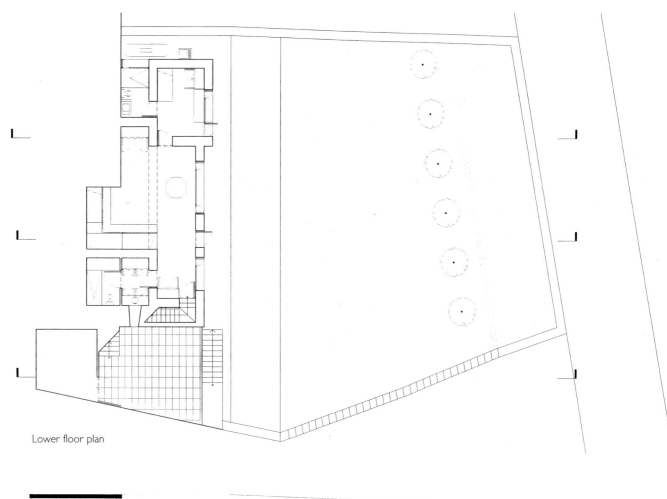

Lower floor plan

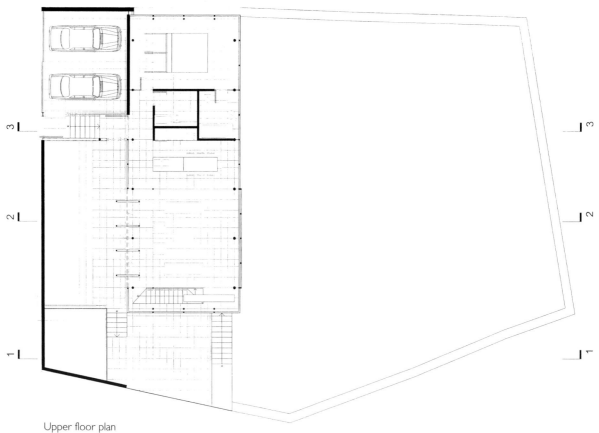

Upper floor plan

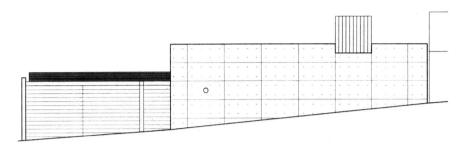

A blind retaining wall forms the facade that faces the street and also contains the swimming pool. This wall in turn supports a wooden wall placed above street level, inside which the water tank is located. The house is therefore suspended in a fragile balance between two bodies of water, the pool and the lake.

North facade

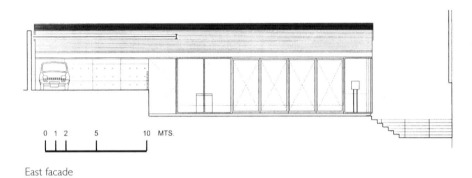

0 1 2   5   10   MTS.

East facade

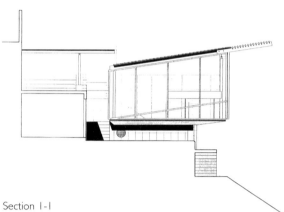

Section 1-1

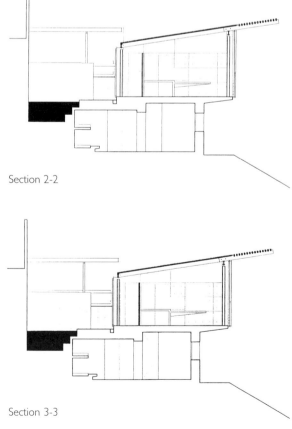

Section 2-2

Section 3-3

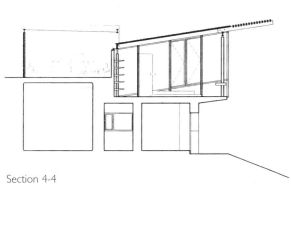

Section 4-4

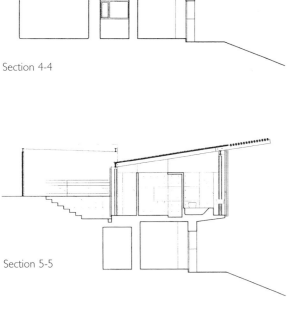

Section 5-5

Linda Searl, Joseph Valerio
Ohio House

Chicago, Illinois, USA

The streets are the essence of the city. They are a community symbol, a place of encounter. In them lies the tension, even the violence. The urban streets encapsulate everything that we cannot find in the suburbs: light, energy and activity. In a city like Chicago, with such a clear grid plan, the crossroads are critical. It could be said that everything happens at the corners.

Instead of being articulated axially toward each of the streets that converge at a point, the Ohio Street House takes as its axis the same point, the corner, capturing the energy that concentrates at the intersection of the grid.

The design of this dwelling is based on two superimposed forms: a circle and a square that share the same centroid. The dwelling is at the same time open and defensive. On one hand, the construction reflects the discipline of the street; on the other, it receives and absorbs all the unexpected events that happen in it. Highly expressive materials were used in the construction of the house, underlining the division between the ground floor and the upper floors. The lower level has a brickwork cladding which does not contrast with the surrounding dwellings. On the upper floors, however, the exterior was clad in grooved metal plates. The facade that gives onto the street seems to be a continuation of that of the ground floor, but the rear part of the dwelling is solved in a different way, in a semicircle.

In the house, the more public elements of the floor plan are developed in parallel to the two streets that form the corner. The living room is aligned with Oakley Street and curves to form the space devoted to the kitchen and dining room, parallel to Ohio Street. Inside this "L" is the staircase. The public spaces are located in the corner giving onto the street, while the private environments are located in the opposite corner. The central staircase leads to the upper levels. The first floor houses the main bedroom, a dressing room and the main bathroom. The second floor houses a bedroom, a bathroom and a large work area.

Photographs: Barbara Karant/Karant+Associates

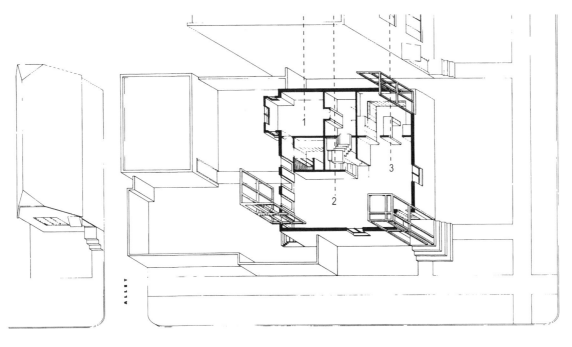

Axonometric view
1. Study
2. Living
3. Dining

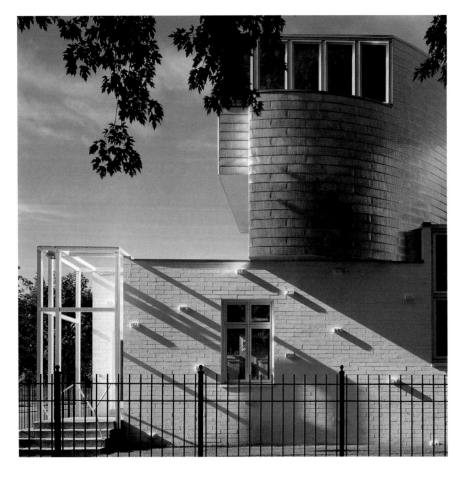

First floor plan

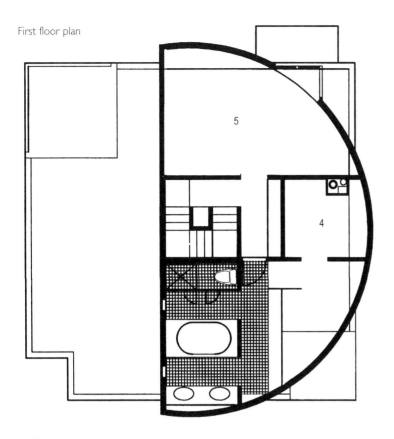

1. Bedroom
2. Workroom
3. Void
4. Closet
5. Bedroom

Second floor plan

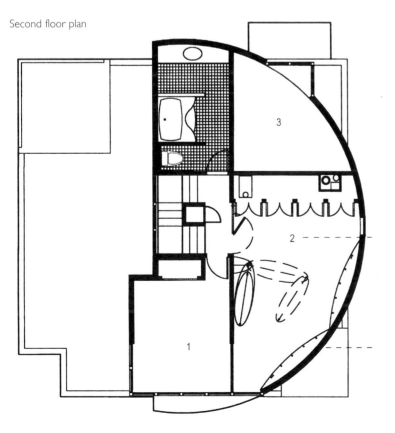

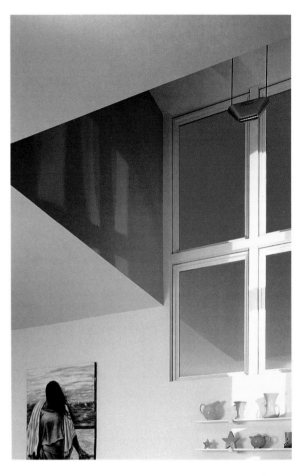

David Adjaye Associates
Elektra House

London, UK

The client, a sculptor with two small children, desired a flexible home which would contain a space in which to work as well as live. The program made use of the existing boundary walls and foundations. A new steel frame was inserted, from which hang the facades, allowing a small load to be transferred onto the existing footings.

The front of the house faces north and is conceived as an insulated facade with no outside views. This mute elevation is expressed in the interior as a double-height space with a continuous skylight running the length of the house, acting as a light chimney for the flexible live/work space on the ground.

The back of the house faces south and enjoys the full east to west aspect. This is exploited by making a large glazed clerestory and reflecting wall, creating a second double-height space, which scoops sunlight into the ground floor. The lower part of the elevation is divided into two: on one side is a glazed box and on the other a concertina window system opens onto a walled court space.

The upper floor is entered on the east side by a maple staircase. Upstairs, the rooms are small but the floor to ceiling heights are deliberately tall (3.2 meters). Each room has a full height door, which is the same thickness as the wall construction, and a skylight which is positioned to reflect as much light into the rooms as possible. The skylights are inclined in a specific direction resulting in a clock-like effect.

Photographs: Lyndon Douglas

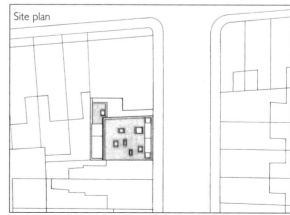

Site plan

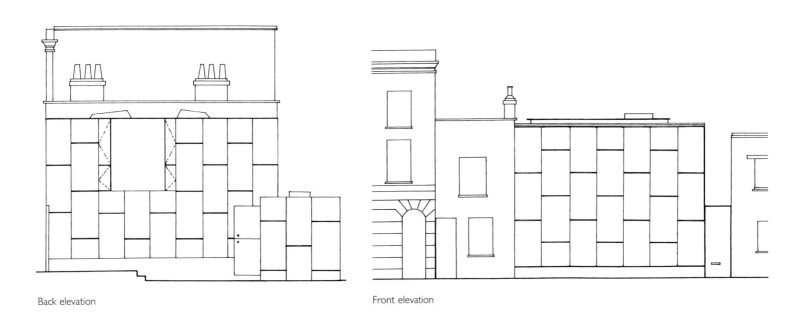

Back elevation

Front elevation

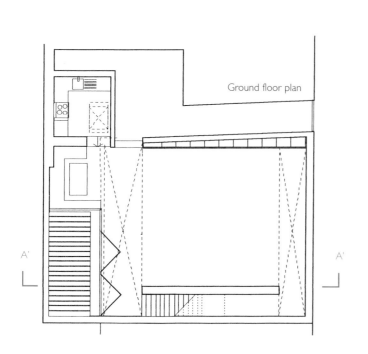

Ground floor plan

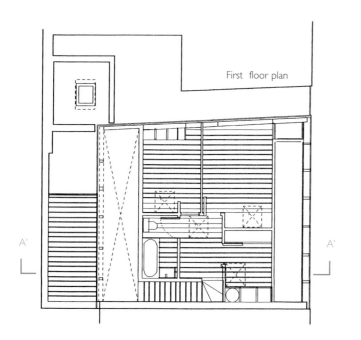

First floor plan

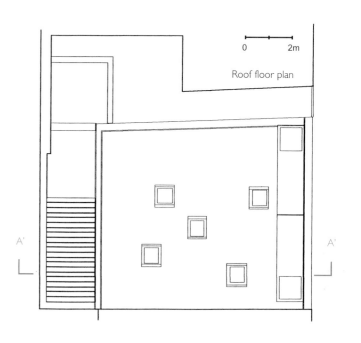

0   2m

Roof floor plan

On the south facade, 4x1-meter double glazed units are glued into aluminum frames, running to the top of the parapet, and are held by a steel I-section beam which runs the length of the house.

Back elevation

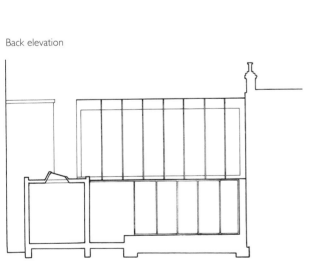

Section A-A

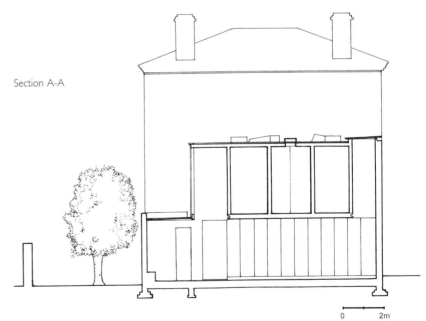

0   2m

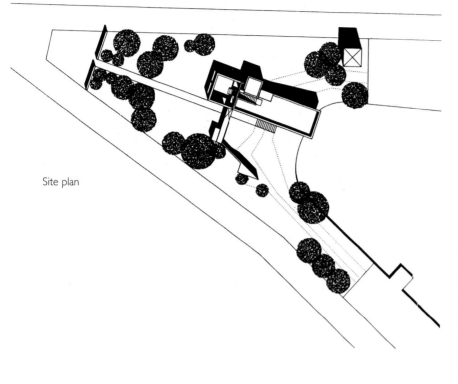

Site plan

Ernst Beneder
House HUF

Blindenmarkt, Austria

Conceived as a weekend refuge for a couple of doctors, this small dwelling located in the proximity of Vienna, next to the towns of Linz and Amstetten in lower Austria, is developed inside a prismatic wooden volume that rises above the water, thereby relating two elements of the landscape: the artificial pond in front of it and a small clearing in the damp nearby forest. The first view is the image of the water framed by the garden wall and the longitudinal volume of the house.

The building clings to the site over the slope of the land, marking a layout with strong geometric rigor. The long wooden volume floats above the land; its eastern half resting on a concrete plinth that is inserted in the slope surrounding the pond.

The opposite façade sits firmly on the land and, in its interior, a courtyard is closed off by the embrace of the outer façade walls. Thus, the architecture refers first to its environment: its position in relation to the pond, which is a reciprocal object of its location, and beyond.

The interior is a single space featuring the living room, which occupies the space corresponding to the overhang over the pond from which a large double window offers splendid views. Access to this environment is through the kitchen.

A narrow access path that starts from the vertex of the site leads along the south facade to the large opening of the entrance. This road is prolonged by an external stairway that ends in the water and gives access to the cellar located in the plinth.

Photographs: Margherita Spiluttini

The dwelling was conceived as a simple elongated wooden box that opens selectively onto the surrounding landscape.

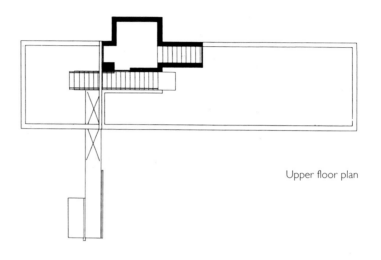

Upper floor plan

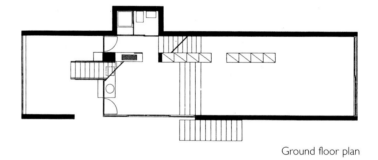

Ground floor plan

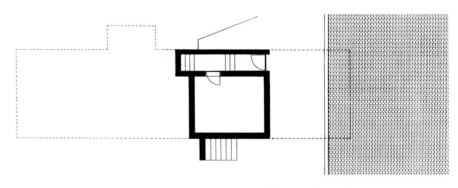

Basement floor plan

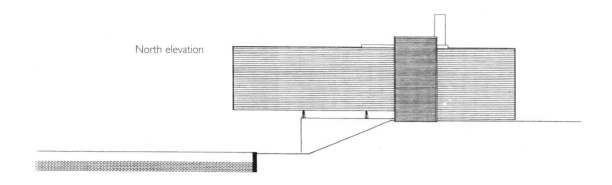

North elevation

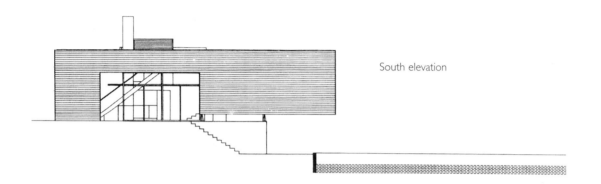

South elevation

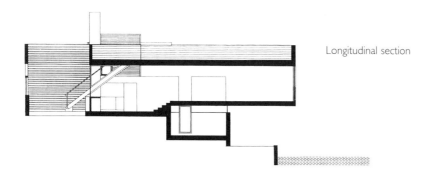

Longitudinal section

From the courtyard the roof terrace can be reached by a light metal staircase.

The dwelling opens onto the magnificent landscape that surrounds it through a totally glazed wall on the east side.

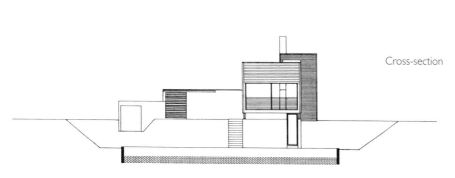

Cross-section

José Cruz Ovalle
Study and Home in Vitacura

Santiago, Chile

This scheme is located in a neighborhood consisting of single-family dwellings surrounded by large gardens. The area was developed fifty years ago near the river Mapocho, which crosses the city of Santiago from east to west. At the present time the neighborhood has been consolidated and occupies a relatively central position in the city.

The 665-m² site is flanked by a single-family dwelling converted into a store and another dwelling whose garden has an area of approximately one hectare. Inside it stand two separate buildings -the street-side studio and the dwelling at the rear- with a garden-courtyard between them.

The front garden is treated as a public space: it is not fenced off as is habitual in the neighborhood, so the studio has a public rather than a domestic character.

The studio is placed crossways on the site occupying the total width, so its interior space extends on two fronts: toward the street and toward the garden-courtyard of the dwelling. The interior is developed so that there is a complete and flowing perspective of the internal space from any angle - it is an interior in which to linger. This is achieved by retaining the internal void through the articulation of depth without creating a vanishing point. Wooden surfaces fold and unfold to temper the light without producing shade or glare on the work surfaces. Openings and interstices are carefully angled to receive the different types of light entering from different directions according to the time of day and the season.

On the other side, the dwelling, situated at the rear of the site facing the northern sun, opens up toward the garden-courtyard between the two buildings. The volume of the studio, located in front of the house, closes this space and prevents a vanishing point toward the street.

It is habitual in Santiago to enter houses from the street, cross them and end up in a living room in front of the garden. This is a way of conceiving space on the basis of the direction. But in this house the order is inverted because one enters the living room from the garden.

The architect did not start from isolated directions but tried to redirect the space, managing the depth and controlling the vanishing point. Thus, for example, the arrangement of the diagonal walls in the living room and the thickness between the pillars and the plane of the windows opens a transverse depth that continues through the trees, grass and bushes to the facade of the studio.

Because the openings through which the light penetrates the house are much larger, dark wooden parquet was used for the horizontal plane of the floor, in order for it to absorb and control the luminosity. With this system the furniture, the objects and the building itself do not receive the light reflected from the floor, which gives them a more solid and settled image.

Photographs: Juan Purcell

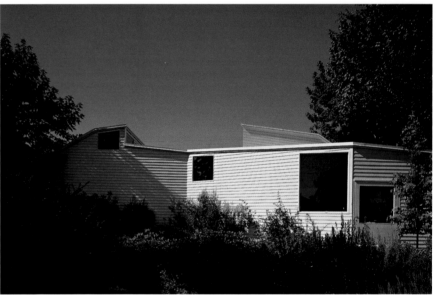

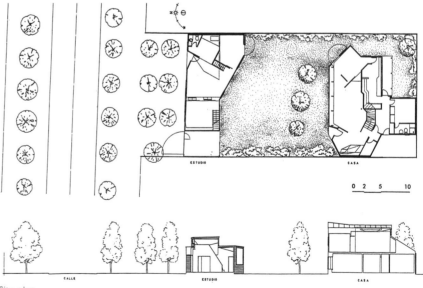

Site plan

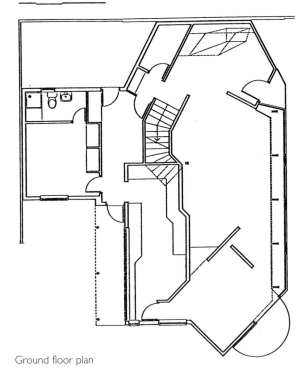

Ground floor plan

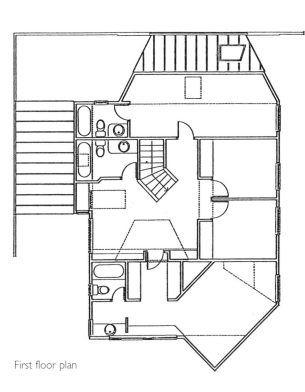

First floor plan

The two parts of the project are placed at the ends of the site, separated by a garden.

Longitudinal section

0 1   2.5   5

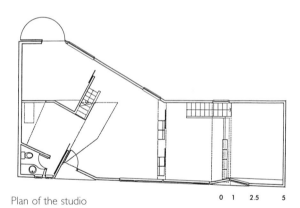

Plan of the studio

0 1   2.5   5

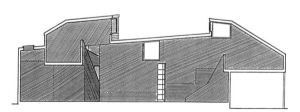

Longitudinal section of the studio

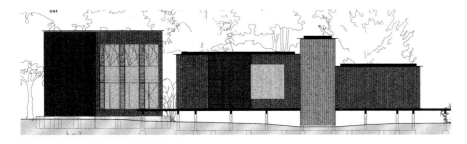

Dieter Thiel
Bangert and House

Schopfheim, Germany

This German publisher's office on the slopes of an old orchard in the Black Forest is made of wood in the traditional way, but is entirely modern in design, technology and ecological awareness. The two buildings, while sharing the site with a house from the 50s, are completely divorced from it and each other and positioned with due regard to a fine stock of old trees.

They are a shining example of the future-oriented design both ecologically and structurally. They also pay due heed to the client's demand for a clearly readable timbered house architecture with variable lighting conditions, excellent indoor climate and perfect acoustics.

The major one of the two new structures (studio and library) comprises three differently dimensioned "wooden boxes" on an open plan so that, given the complete absence of partitions, the open cluster offers a room of great visual tension measuring 17.6 meters in length and having three different widths and heights. The other new cube rising obliquely positioned at some distance from it on a 7.2 m² floor plan functions as a two-story guest house.

As opposed to conventional timbered houses it features the fundamental difference of having uncompromisingly materialized the idea of a building severely devoid of extra finishing work, such as cladding and lining. The system complied at once with the client's demand that individual cubes be prefabricated on a maximum scale to achieve an optimum of high-grade workmanship and a minimum of in-situ installation time.

Photographs: Klaus Frahm / Contur

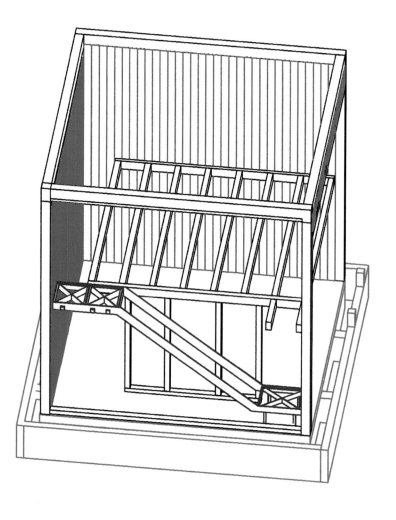

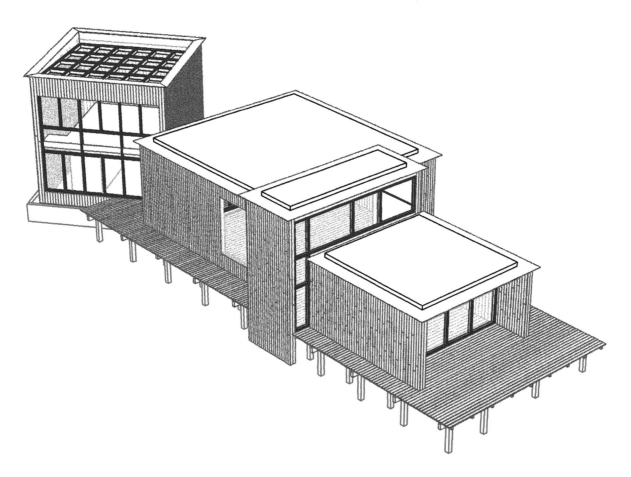

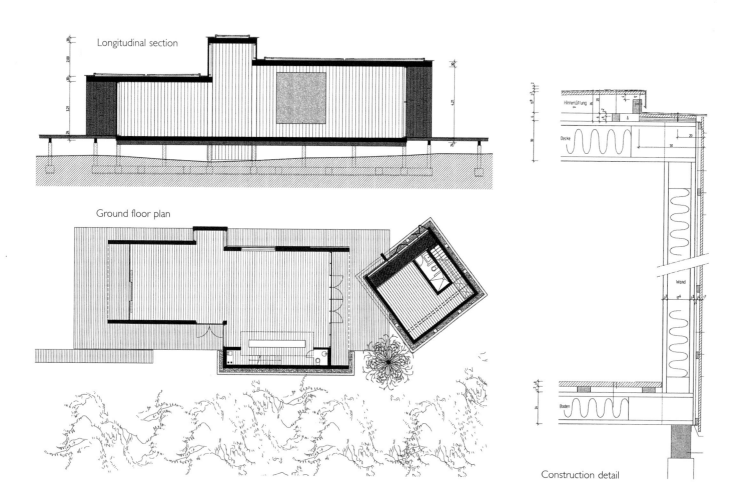

Longitudinal section

Ground floor plan

Construction detail

Ushida Findlay Partnership
Polyphony

Osaka, Japan

Located on a site in a suburb of Osaka created for the Exhibition of 1970, this original dwelling was conceived for a couple of musicians and their children. Music and architecture seem to converge in this building, which bears a certain resemblance to the structure of the inner ear.

Polyphony is a musical term that refers to the overlapping of sounds in a composition. Authors like Bartok, who incorporated popular songs in his works, and John Cage, who introduced the sound created by the public and the space, paved the way for contemporary music, which uses sampling and mixes to create sound atmospheres full of superimposed nuances.

The combination of sound and construction has a long tradition in Japan, where materials and vegetation (such as bamboo to transform the wind into music and attract birds) are often chosen for the acoustic effect that they give. In the design of this dwelling, conceived so that its inhabitants could experience the sounds of the environment as part of a total sensorial experience, the aim was to create a space that had a correlation with the repetitive acoustic cycles.

The ground plan of the dwelling is based on a geometric pattern on which circles of 3.4 m in diameter are traced around a main circle, achieving an original form similar to that of a slightly curved sausage. This winding tube is cut diagonally, so that the solid is gradually transformed into a void. The overlapping of cylinders to generate a space of multiple layers is directly related to the effect of the chords formed by superimposed sounds.

In accordance with the visual experience of the space, it was intended to create a sound landscape in which it was possible to experience a range of unexpected acoustic effects. This was achieved by means of curved walls forming a series of corridors that seem to whisper and give off strange echoes as if one held a shell to one's ear. These curved forms are repeated in the whole house and make the interior an enveloping place full of winding corners in which the furniture and the openings play a major role.

Photographs: Katsuhisa Kida, Takeshi Taira

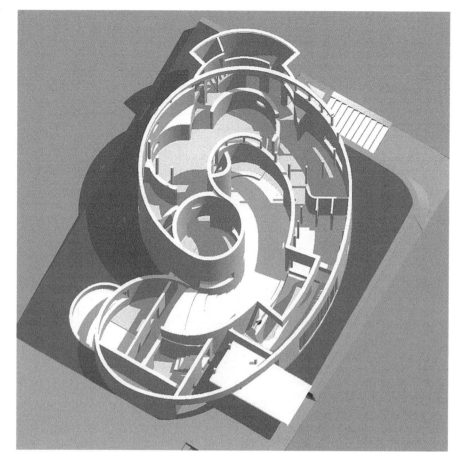

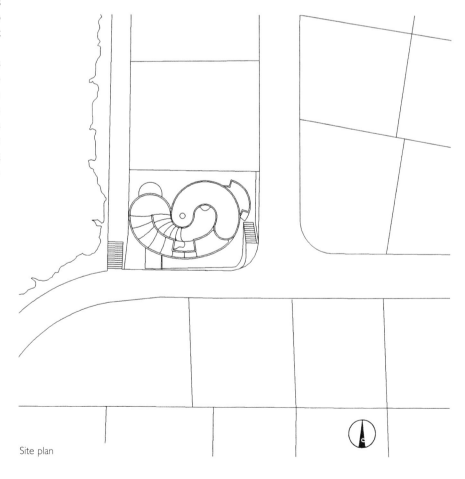

Site plan

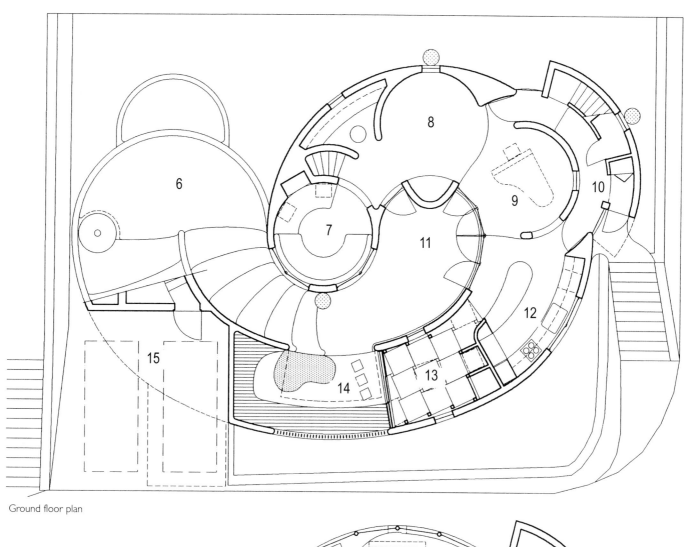

Ground floor plan

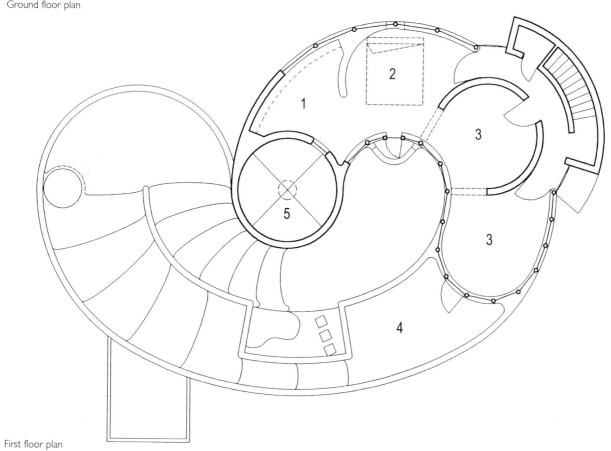

First floor plan

The ground plan of the dwelling is based on a geometric pattern on which circles of 3.4 m diameter are traced around a main circle. This creates a winding, tubular space that appears to be cut diagonally so that the solid is gradually transformed into a void.

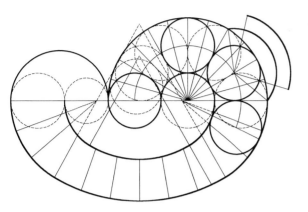

1. Wardrobe
2. Main bedroom
3. Bedroom
4. Terrace
5. Void
6. Kids patio
7. Audio zone
8. Family zone
9. Piano zone
10. Entrance
11. Courtyard
12. Kitchen-dining
13. Japanese room
14. Garden
15. Garage
16. Bathroom

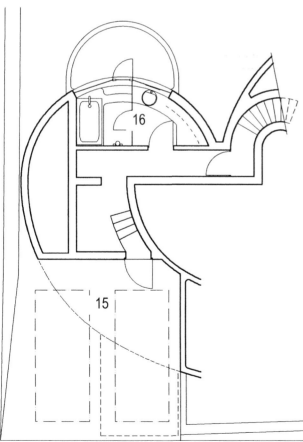

Basement floor plan

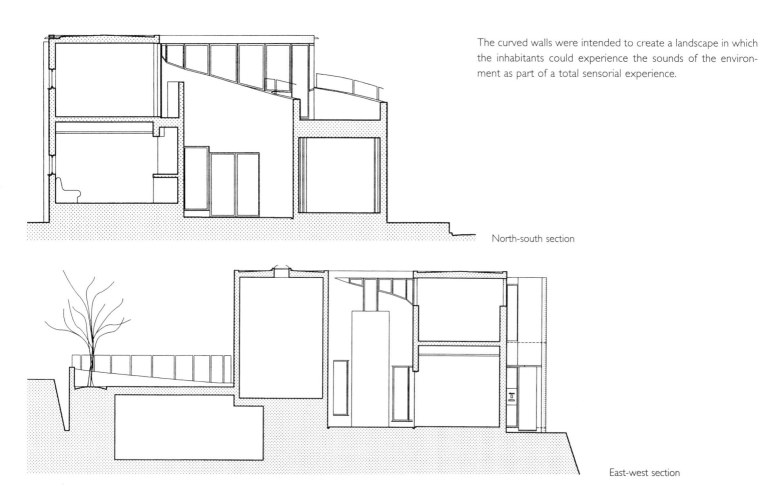

The curved walls were intended to create a landscape in which the inhabitants could experience the sounds of the environment as part of a total sensorial experience.

North-south section

East-west section

210

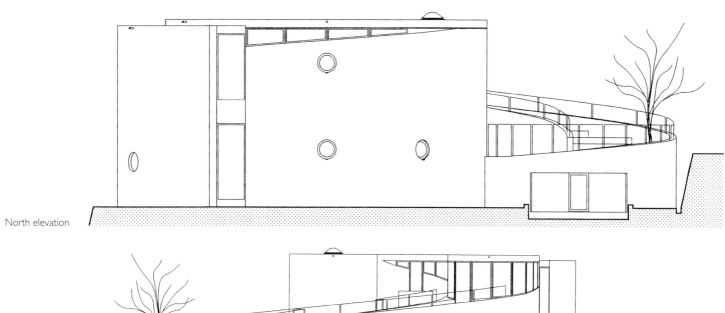

North elevation

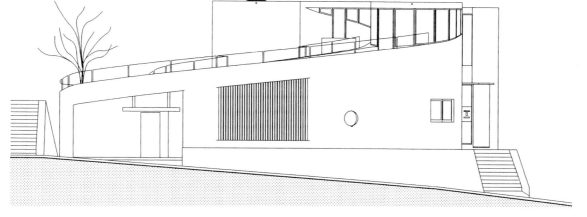

South elevation

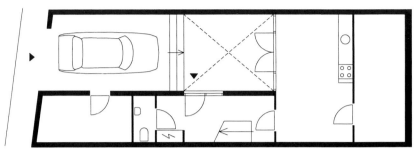

Ground floor plan

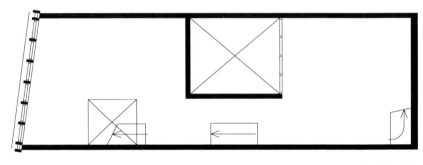

First floor plan

Claus & Kaan
Draaisma Private Apartment

Amsterdam, The Netherlands

The urban design for the surrounding area of Borneo-Sporenburg, two peninsulas in the eastern harbor of Amsterdam, was done by West 8 / Adriaan Geuze. The importance of this particular scheme lies in the fact that it offers an urban alternative to the modernist low-rise garden city extensions that spread insidiously, taking up a lot of space, offering no urban quality whilst perverting the original housing typology because the individual houses and gardens are becoming smaller.

The program consists of 1400 houses in a very high, inner city-like density. Although the houses have no gardens, open spaces cut into the volume, offering absolute privacy. To meet the project ends, several architects were chosen to work on the same typology: the introverted individual house.

Photographs: Christian Richters

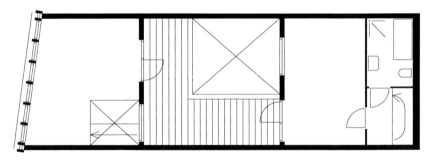

Second floor plan

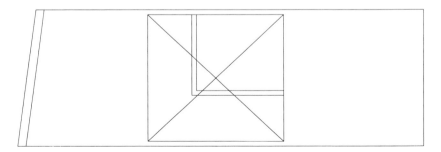

Roof plan

Although the houses have no garden, each one has a central space that acts as an atrium around which the scheme is developed.

The design of these dwellings was based on the desire to give the space width and brightness. The absence of unnecessary partitions helps to create dynamic and flexible spaces, while the generous and carefully studied use of glazed surfaces creates a dialogue between interior and exterior.

215

Elevations

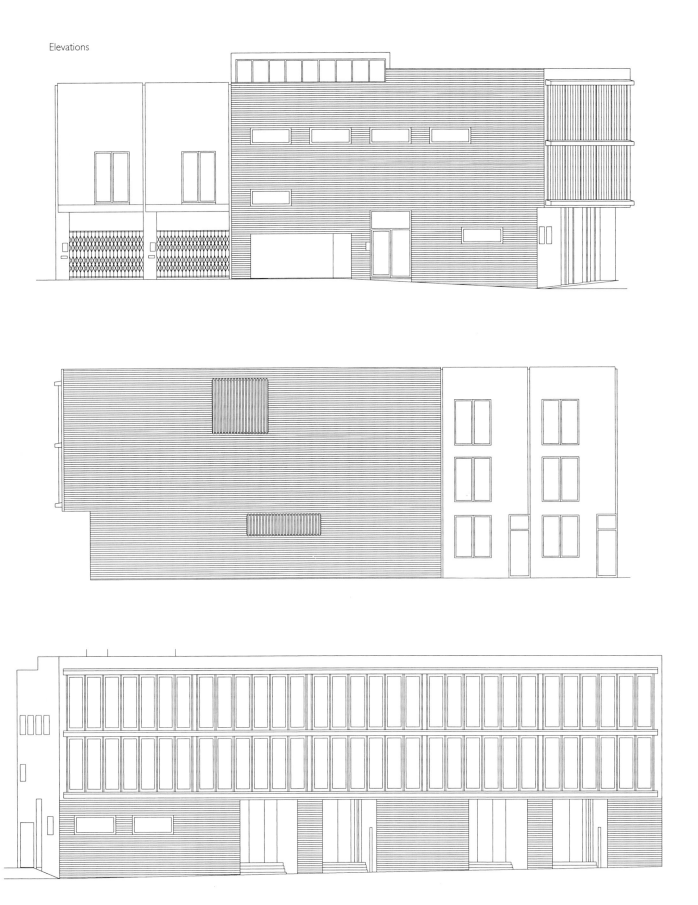

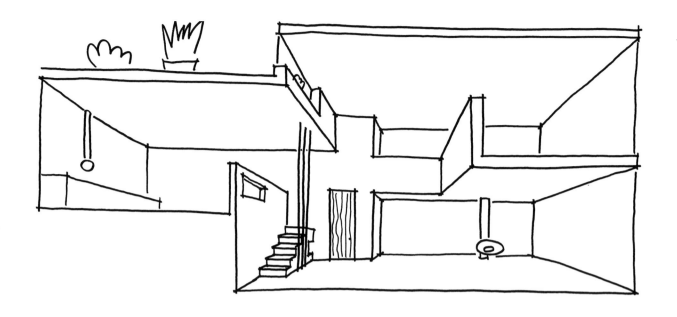

Cross section

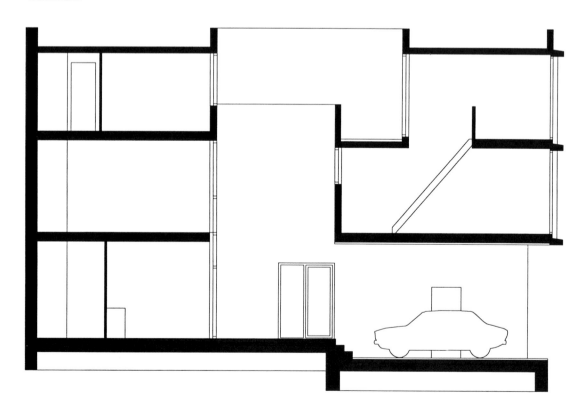

Tod Williams, Billie Tsien
Rifkind House

Long Island, New York, USA

The clients, a life-long city dwelling professional couple with grown children, had never owned a car or a house; thus, the design and construction of this house held great significance for them. It is to serve as a weekend retreat, a place for them both to work and a compound for the children, spouses and future grandchildren. It is to be a place apart; an antidote to the intensity of their lives in New York, a refuge in which to enjoy their desire for peace and quiet.

The site by a pond and with distant views of the ocean is approached on foot because the parking has been pulled away from the house. Organized in three volumes on one level, one enters a courtyard suggested by the placement of the buildings. The house is not air-conditioned but takes advantage of cross-breezes and a site which has beautiful pitch pines and complete separation from any neighbors.

The three pavilions of the program have been configured so that each room frames a different view and enjoys its own access to the landscape. The central block contains the kitchen with living room on one side and dining on the other, and a small reading loft above. The master bedroom, dressing bath and study are separate and may be occupied independently from the third block, which may also be occupied independently. This third block contains three bedrooms for children and guests. A smaller volume is a storage and refuse shed.

The house is wood frame with cedar siding and Douglas fir lining the interior of solid exterior walls. Windows are mahogany. Floors are Douglas fir and New York bluestone in honed and split face, as is the chimney. Built-in bookshelves, beds, dressers and custom furniture are of American cherry.

The architects' desire was to design a house which finds its place and meaning though a careful choreography with the existing trees, balancing form and nature. Its integral relationship to the landscape and light allows the house to transform over the course of the changing days and seasons.

Photographs: Michael Moran

The pavilions that form the dwelling are distributed on the site in a very rational way. Their layout guarantees the maximum use of natural light.

The central volume that houses the public areas of the house has a glazed facade that permits total communication between interior and exterior. The lantern windows accentuate the verticality of the space and establish a rhythm in the living room.

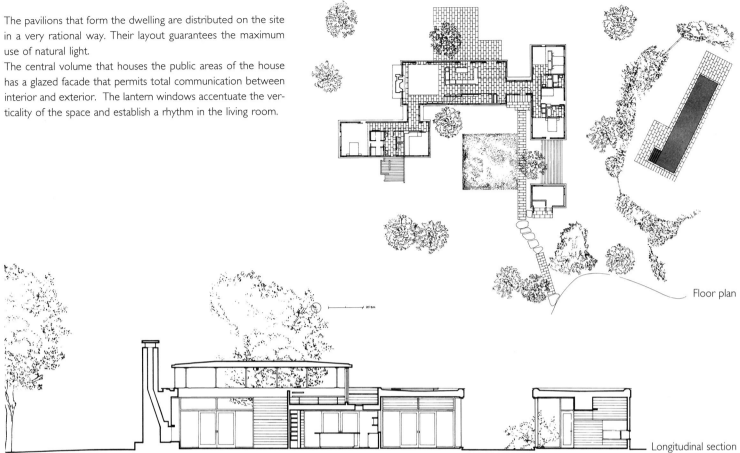

Floor plan

Longitudinal section

223

Kunihide Oshinomi & Takeshi Semba
Timber Frame House with a Curtain Wall

Shinagawa-ku, Tokyo, Japan

The ideas governing the structural design of this four-story house derive from having seen the tragic spectacle of the destruction of timber houses in the Kobe earthquake and as a result of a close collaboration between the architects and a structural engineer specializing in high-rise buildings.

The site for this project was of an irregular, truncated triangle shape. A retaining wall was on the side by the boundary wall and timber was on the other side.

The bearing strength of the ground was not sufficient for concrete construction and, because of fire safety regulations, a steel frame construction would have required fire-proof cladding. Yet, if timber-panel construction had been chosen, it would have been difficult to make large openings.

Amid such constraints, the framework that was decided upon was a semi-rigid structure of reinforced concrete, glue-laminated timber frame with metal fittings, and a wooden bearing wall. In order to keep the north and east sides open to the site's more attractive views, the bearing walls are placed on the south and west faces. The north face, now free of cumbersome structural elements, is a curtain wall with double glazing of clear float glass. Also, by pre-cutting the glue-laminated wood and providing metal joint fittings, a very precise and unrestricted structure was created, while also cutting down on construction time.

In the interior, Japanese beech flooring with a urethane-coat finish creates a cozy atmosphere.

Photographs: Van Structural Design

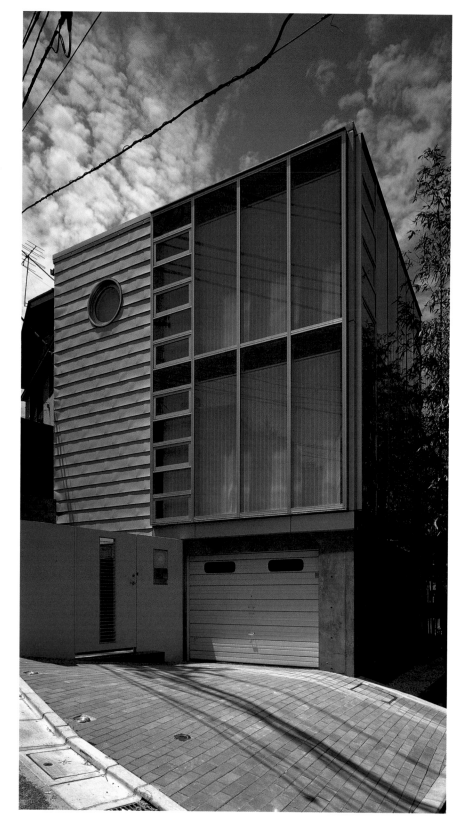

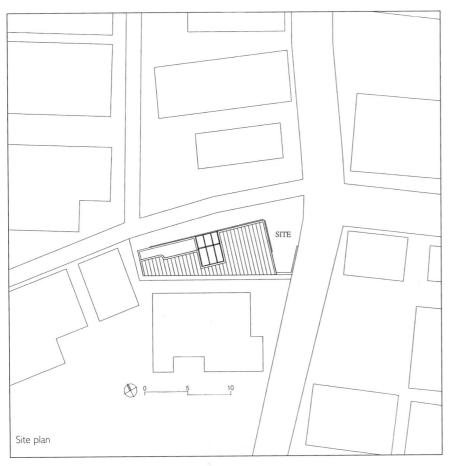

Site plan

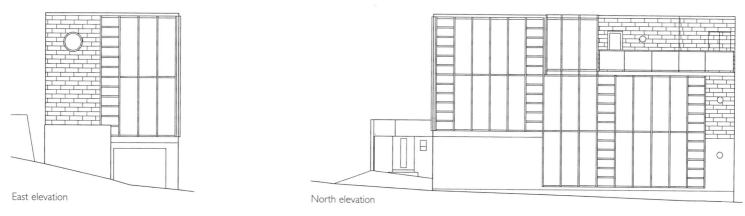

East elevation

North elevation

228

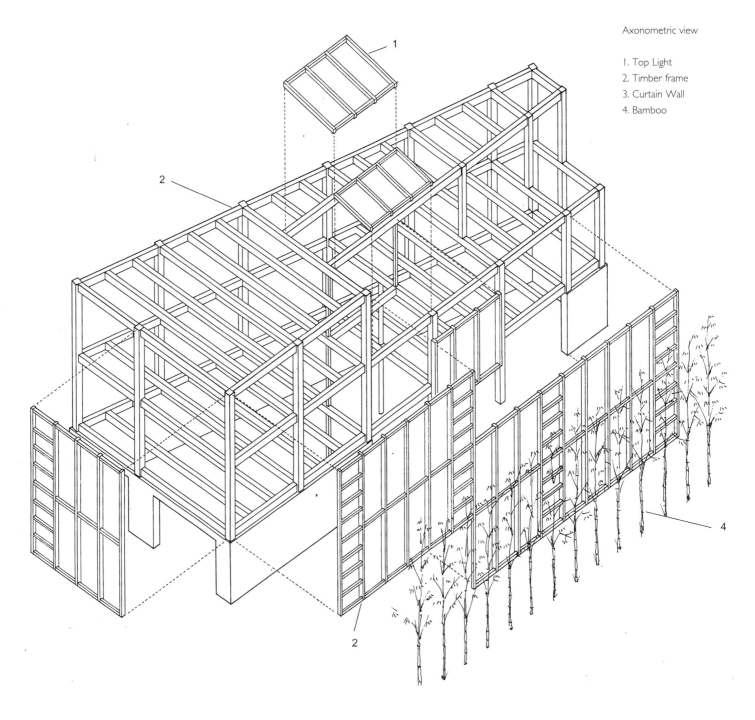

Axonometric view

1. Top Light
2. Timber frame
3. Curtain Wall
4. Bamboo

229

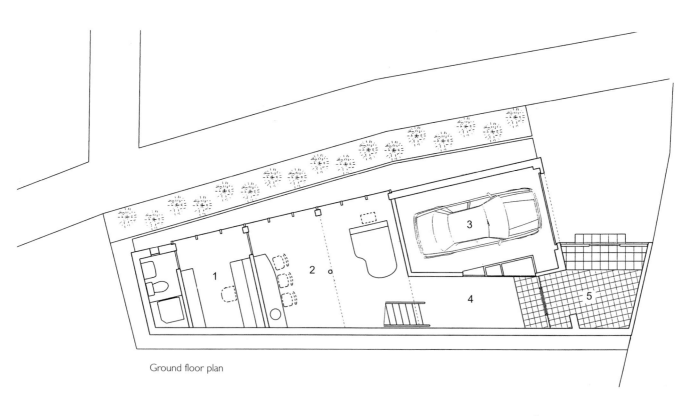

Ground floor plan

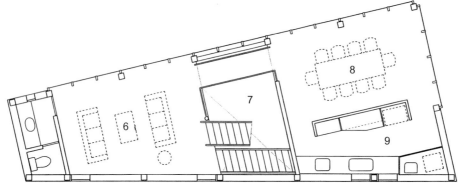

First floor plan

1. Study
2. Hall
3. Garage
4. Entrance
5. Porch
6. Living room
7. Void
8. Dining room
9. Kitchen
10. Terrace
11. Bath
12. Closet
13. Main bedroom
14. Bedroom

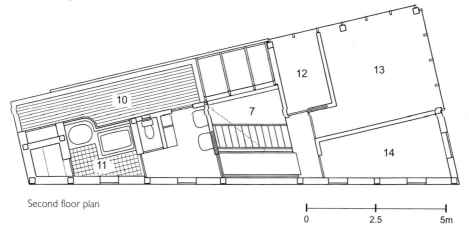

Second floor plan

0   2.5   5m

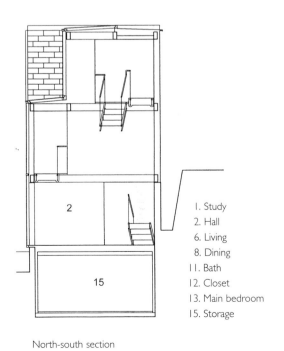

1. Study
2. Hall
6. Living
8. Dining
11. Bath
12. Closet
13. Main bedroom
15. Storage

North-south section

East-west section

0   2.5   5

13   12   11

8   6

3   2   1

15

The north face enjoys floor-to-ceiling double glazing, made possible by having placed the bearing walls on the south and east sides. Japanese beech wood flooring provides a warm contrast to aluminum and painted steel rails and stairs.

J. A. Martínez Lapeña & Elías Torres
Vicenç Marí House

Ibiza, Spain

This project was for a house in Santa Eulalia, Ibiza. The wish, shared by the clients and the architect alike, to preserve the surrounding landscape resulted in a design, which would limit the building to the space required to fulfill the basic needs. The idea was to occupy a precisely defined space and, outside of its boundaries, to leave no more lasting mark than that left by the car, which, like an umbilical chord, connects the dwelling to the public road. The living area inside is protected: the patios -closed off from outside views- are outcroppings of the walls. Wings stretch outward and upward to gather the temporary divisions between the terraces and interior spaces within their fold, as well as to capture the sun.

The image of the house recalls a private triple-deck boat sailing in search of the south, moored amidst Mediterranean pine trees. On closer inspection, one manages to discern the old family home with its crops.

The pool is a huge bath in a roofless room enclosed by the home's walls, in effect a room with water. It is raised above the terrace floor, just as the cistern of old were elevated above fields, so that while on the terrace only the reflections on the walls hint at its presence. One of the walls is dyed indigo blue, the color of a glass of water. The pool is concrete, also indigo blue, and finished with a cream-colored limestone crest. Glimpses of the landscape can be caught while swimming and splashing about in the pool, whose surface is 21.25 m².

Photographs: Duccio Malagamba

Ground floor plan

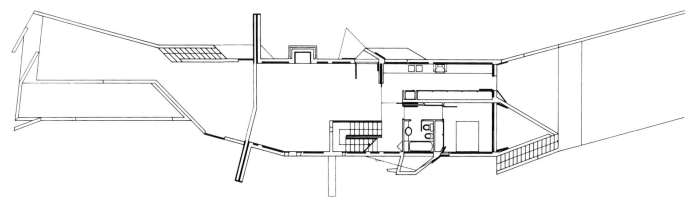

First floor plan

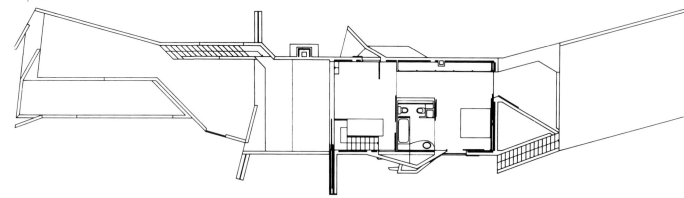

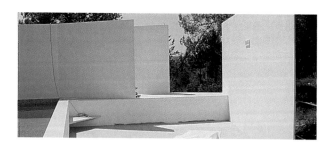

East elevation

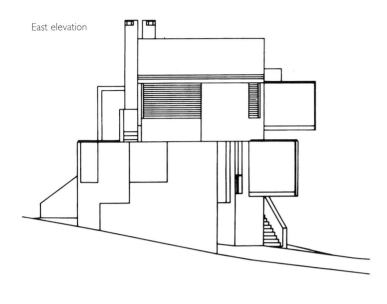

West elevation

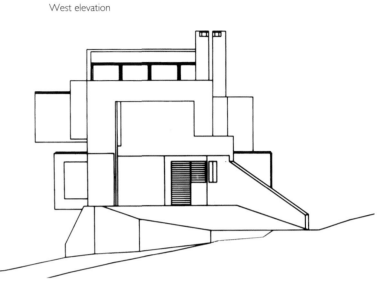

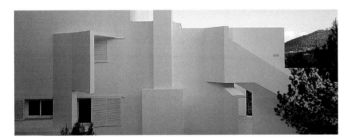

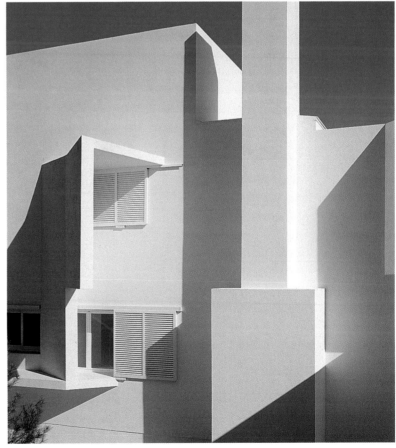

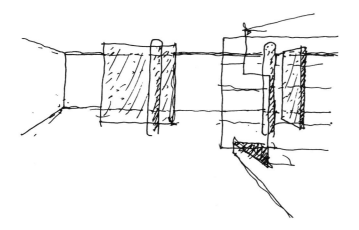

Thomas Hanrahan & Victoria Meyers
Holley Loft

New York, USA

This project is an adaptation of an existing 4000 ft2 industrial loft space into a residence. The space is on the second floor of a loft building in lower Manhattan. In the final design, no solid walls were left. A single full-height wall of glass and steel marked the major division of master bedroom and bathroom from the rest of the apartment. From any position, the intention is to experience the full dimension of the entire loft space, with all the elements of the program distributed freely in the form of low cabinetry and movable panels. This disposition yields a complex space of constantly changing perspectives and points of view. Light from the short ends of the apartment penetrates deep into the residence, while the movable panels allow for the creation of smaller, more intimate spaces to accommodate overnight guests.

The major division within the space is made by a 48ft long raw steel and glass wall. This marks the division between the master bedroom/master bath area and the rest of the apartment with sandblasted areas for privacy. The area covered by the curtain is clear glass. The movement of the curtain allows the inhabitant of the space to control its openness.

Opposite the steel and glass wall is a 30ft long maple cabinet, which contains an objectified fragment of the steel and glass wall plane. Here, in order to mark its displacement, the wall curves. This cabinet also marks a boundary between the living spaces and a kitchen/guest bath. Translucent materials hang through a wood cabinet at specific locations to partially reveal the space beyond.

Full-height painted wood panels can either close down the rear of the apartment or remain in a fully open position. When they are open the panels float in the space: closed they demarcate one room; closed further, two rooms. The disposition of these spaces changes throughout the day according to the inhabitants' requirements.

Photographs: Peter Aaron / ESTO

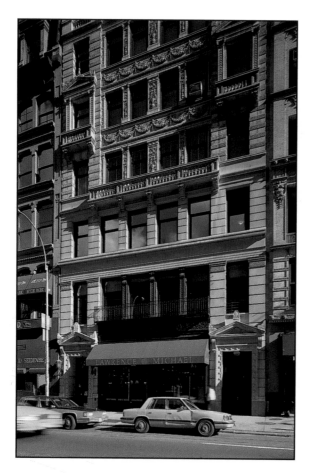

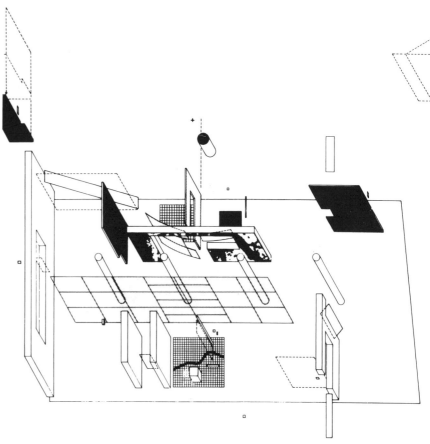

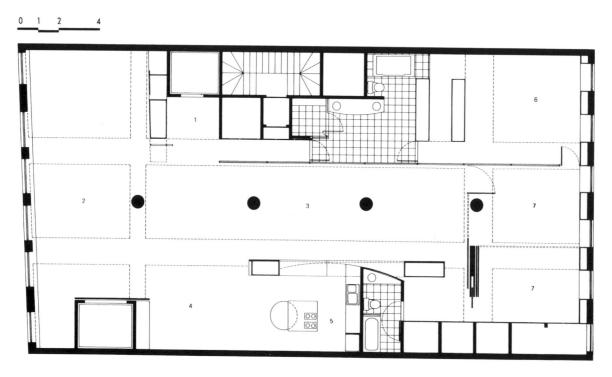

0 1 2   4

Floor plan
1. Entrance
2. Living room
3. Gallery
4. Dining room
5. Kitchen
6. Master bedroom
7. Guest bedroom

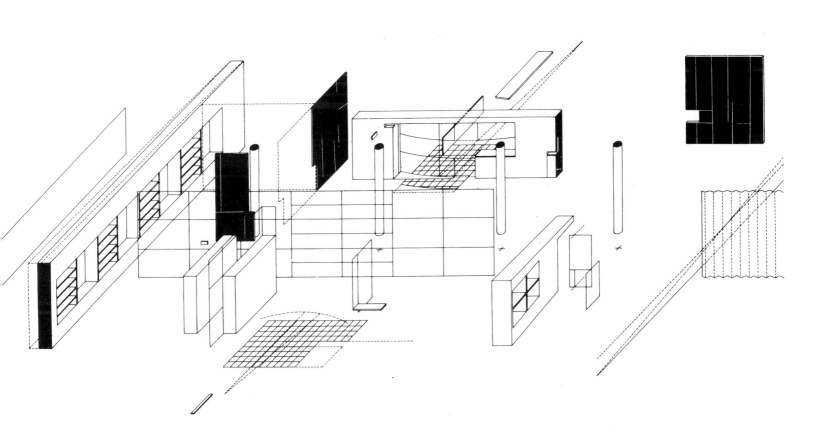

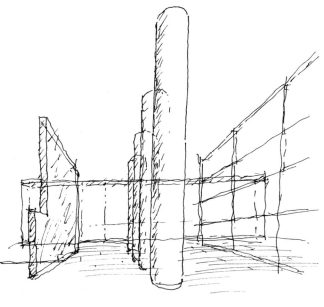

Mark Guard
Apartment in Bankside Lofts
London, UK

This apartment presented several problems. The requirement for two bedrooms, as well as the desire to maximize the living area, was complicated by the relatively low ceiling heights. The only means of providing a satisfactory double-height space was by combining the sleeping platforms with another function.

The master bedroom therefore sits above the dressing area, which is accessed through a large pivoting door. The guest bedroom, adjacent the main entrance, is atop the guest bathroom. The circular stainless steel shower extends into the main living area and provides a sculptural counterpart to the more geometric forms of the master bedroom, with its "Z" shaped bed head. A stone clad staircase provides the route up to the guest sleeping platform, maximising the floor space in the main living area.

The split-level stone bathroom is positioned halfway between the dressing room and the master bedroom above. To allow light from the window in the bathroom to serve both the bedroom and the bathroom; the latter is open plan. However, as the bathroom is on a lower level, it is not visible from the bedroom, and so the perception of space in the bedroom is maximized.

The WC is placed in a circular enclosure with an etched glass top next to the steps leading up to the bathroom. Sliding the curved door automatically activates the lighting and ventilation system.

The floor of the bathroom is like a small landscape, with variyng levels and forms. The limestone floor, which is electrically heated, steps up to the bathroom and then down to form the bath-shower. A custom-designed polished stainless steel swimming pool ladder provides a secondary means of access to the bathroom from the bedroom.

A large sliding canvas screen can be drawn across the main space, effectively sealing the master bed area from the living space. The apartment was designed to adapt easily to forthcoming developments in entertaining technology. A compartment has been let into the suspended ceiling in order to take a television projection unit, which will be displayed on the large 5x3 m sliding screen. In the master bed area, a space has been designated for a flat screen television, enabling new technology to be seamlessly integrated into the apartment with minimum disruption. A concrete pillar, part of the building's original structure, has been left untouched in the main living area.

Photographs: Henry Wilson

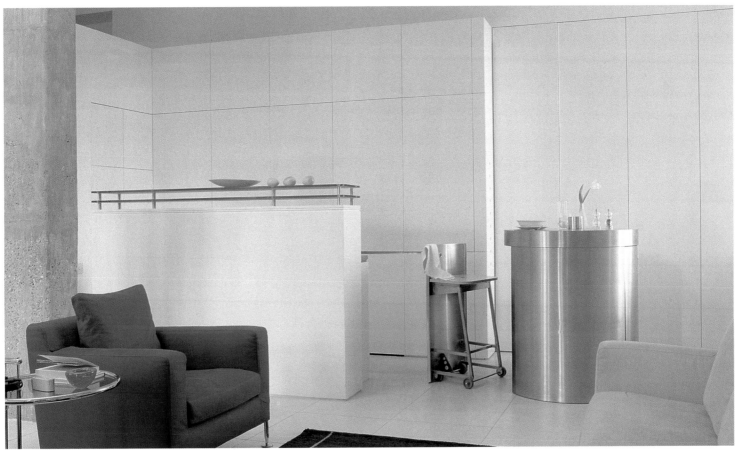

Floor plans

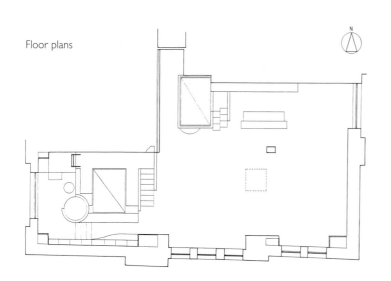

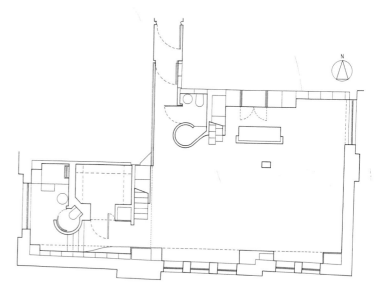

Axonometric views, ground floor plan with projector

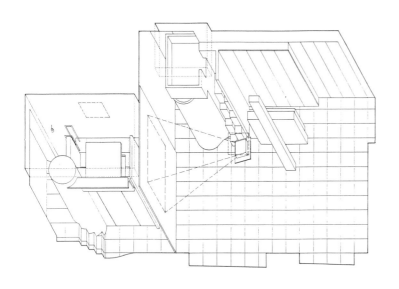

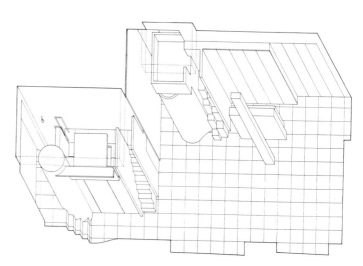

Section

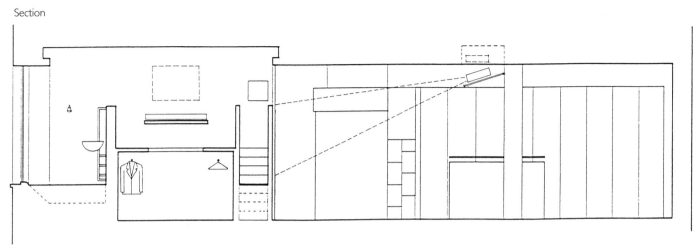

Waro Kishi
House in Higashinada

Kobe, Japan

This house in Higashinada Ward, Kobe, is for a family of two consisting of a mother and a daughter. The conditions are typical for an urban dwelling. There are houses standing close to the site on both sides, and the site configuration is narrow and quite deep. The saving grace of the project is the presence of a park across the street to the north. The design was started with the idea of 'borrowing' the scenery of this park, which penetrates the dwelling through the large glazed openings.

The clients wanted a house in which they could always sense each other's presence. The result is a three-story reinforced concrete house which features one continuous interior space.

The concrete box measures 3.3 meters wide and 16 meters deep and occupies nearly the entire site. The south-western quarter of the box has been made into a light well. There is a split-level arrangement between the northern half of the house and the remaining south-eastern quarter, and interior doors have been provided only where necessary.

The living-dining room on the top floor has a ceiling height of 3.9 meters. It faces the light well in the south-western direction, and stairs with low risers lead, beyond the toplit stairwell, to a terrace half a level above the room in the south-eastern direction. On the north side, windows are extended the full width of the house and provide the interior spaces with views of the trees and grass in the park across the street. This living-dining room is open to both the north and the south. It floats above the city and enables the occupants to enjoy the townscape. Kishi believes that the only thing an urban dwelling has to offer an occupant is an opportunity to enjoy the city.

Photographs: Hiroyuki Hirai

The dwelling has views of a park located to the north. The upper floor, which has a higher ceiling than the rest, thus becomes a semi-open outdoor space.

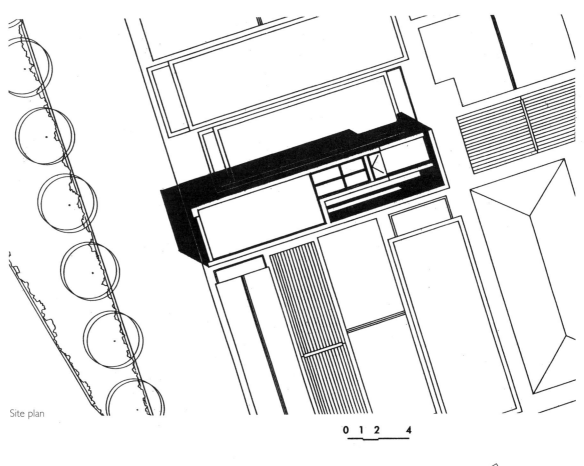

Site plan

0 1 2 4

South elevation

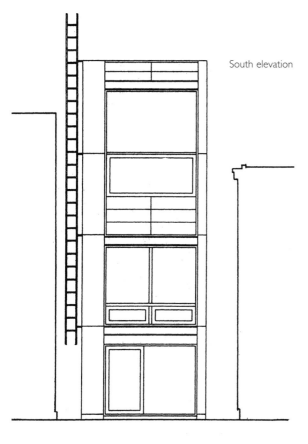

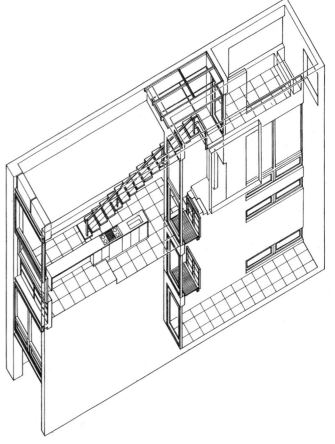

0 0.5 1 2

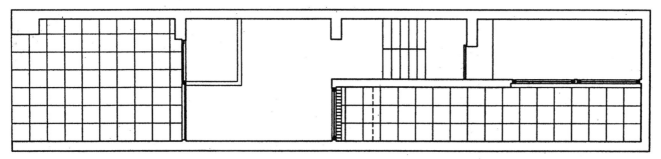

Ground floor plan

The clients wanted a house in which they could always sense each other's presence. The result is a three-story reinforced concrete house, which is one continuous space inside.

The opening of an inner courtyard in the south-west corner of the site provides more light in the house's interior and it increases the sensation of spatial freedom.

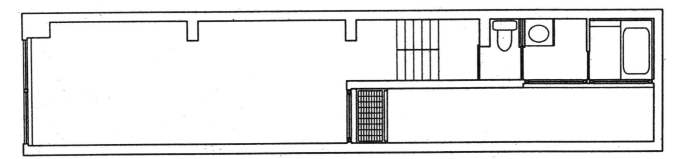

First floor plan

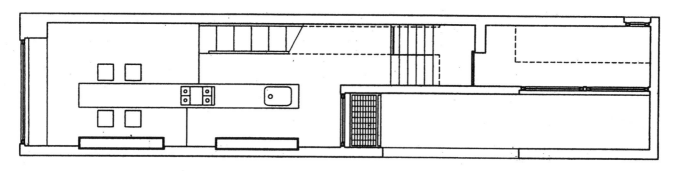

Second floor plan

0 0.5 1 2

The open staircase provides spatial continuity in the vertical direction, transforming the dwelling into a single room fragmented visually into several levels.

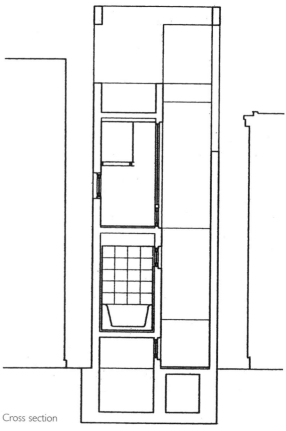

Cross section

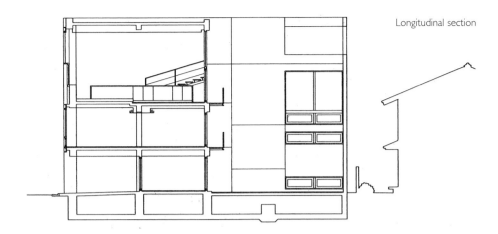

Longitudinal section

259

Pool
In spe-single family house

Wien, Austria

The site is determined on the one hand by a slope falling gently towards the north, and on the other by two statutory regulations restricting the possible building location: it had to be adjoined to the neighboring house and was not allowed to be more than a few meters away from the street on the southern side.

One approaches the house by gentle concrete steps gradually entrenching themselves into the ground, thus leading to the sunken entrance area situated between ground and basement floor. Along with the access steps a car ramp, which, among other things, can also be used as a covered parking space or to play table tennis, runs down to the basement level.

The kitchen/dining area, open completely to the south, is a few steps above entrance level. From this three-meter-high space, four steps lead up to the somewhat lower-height living area, expanding into the garden on the north side. A sliding door provides access to a terrace, beyond which lie a swimming pool and garden.

Turning around again, the slope of the entrance hill leads to a working area situated on top of it, between ground and first floor. Here, sunlight shines into the ground floor, and one has a fair view of the landscape and home.

Another turn, and after some steps one arrives at a small room which provides access to three individual rooms, a bathroom and a small terrace on the south side. From here, a steel stairway leads up to the roof, offering a marvellous view over Lainzerbach.

Photographs: Hertha Hurnaus

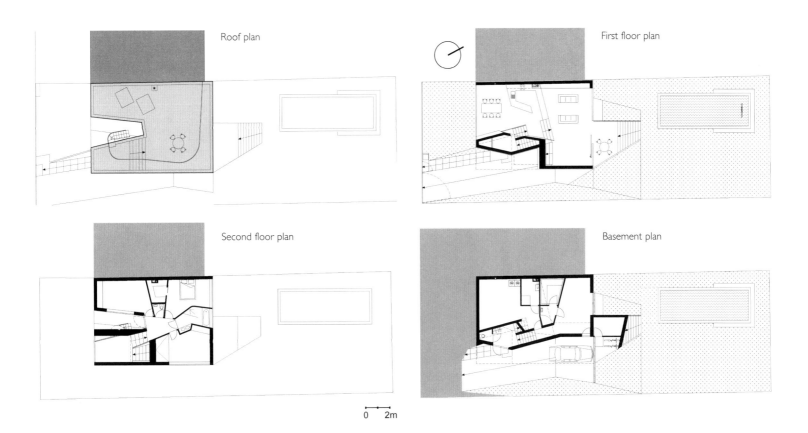

Roof plan

First floor plan

Second floor plan

Basement plan

0   2m

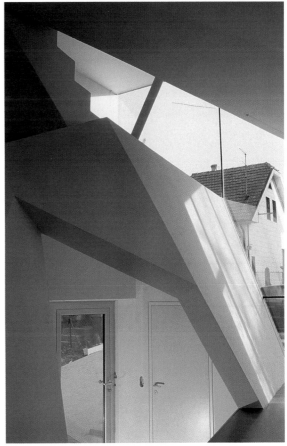

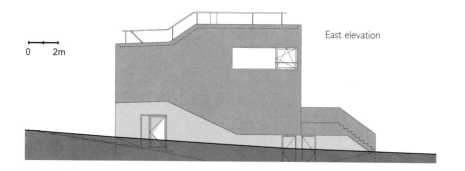

East elevation

0   2m

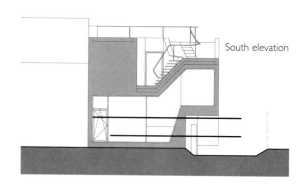

South elevation

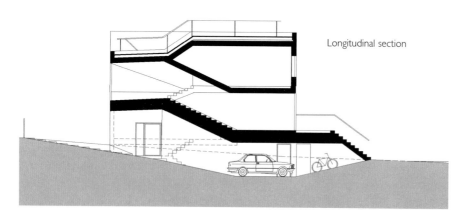

Longitudinal section

The northern and southern elevations are cut open complete-ly, the southern glazed facade flooding the interior with light. Once inside, visitors find themselves in the inside of a cut-up hill, looking down on the one side to the basement, on the other side climbing up into the living area on the ground fllor.

Camagna Camoletto Marcante
Lanzo-Ruggeri House / Lobina House

Turin, Italy

The Casa Lanzo-Ruggeri is a loft located on the fourth floor of an 18th century building in the Baroque center of Turin. The intervention was part of the complete restructuring of the property. The scheme involved the total rehabilitation of the loft, with a floor area of 90 m[2] on two levels. The intervention included the partial replacement of the load-bearing brick structure and the wooden ceiling with a metal system. The aim was to create an apartment with a strong hierarchical organization of the spaces and functions despite the small size of the property.

On the first level, a floating staircase rises opposite the access, where the ceiling is lower. The small section of the metal structure of the ceiling in comparison with the original wooden structure guarantees the maximum habitability of the living room on the upper level.

The kitchen penetrates directly into the living room, from which it is separated by a different type of floor and a different ceiling height. In the lower part of the ceiling a convenient pantry has been recovered. A large glass section is a vehicle for natural and artificial light and also filters the vertical and horizontal relationships between the main rooms.

The Casa Lobina is the dwelling of a couple with a daughter. It occupies 150 m[2] and enjoys privileged views of the Piazza Vittorio Veneto, located in the center of Turin. The scheme involved a minimum intervention in the existing walls, which were treated with the same color as the window frames and floor, thus creating a homogenous container. Slides of the family members are projected in a corridor defined by a series of ochre-coloured glass panels. The house is developed as a sequence of empty rooms that are characterized by the works of art that are exhibited in them. This is a reference to the traditional Japanese dwelling that is devoid of objects but makes up for this with a decorative and changing lighting. This decorative installation acquires a strong architectural value by transcending the pure materiality of a surface for separating atmospheres and becomes a vehicle of dialogue between the physical and virtual spaces that coexist in the house.

Photographs: Emilio Conti

First floor plan

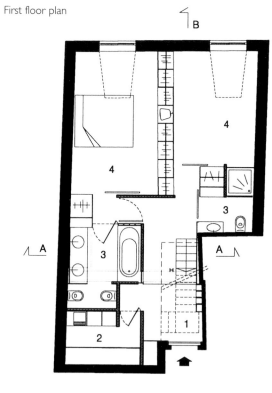

1. Entrance
2. Laundry
3. Bathroom
4. Bedroom

5. Living-dining area
6. Kitchen
7. Pantry

Second floor plan

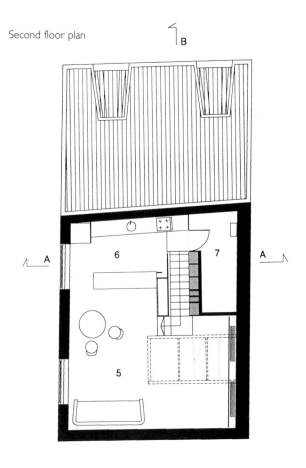

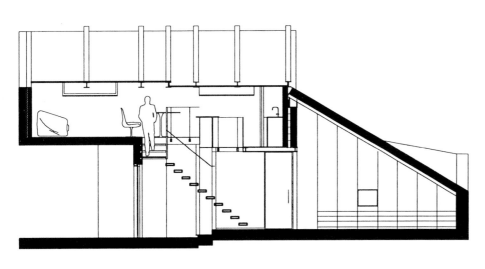

Section B

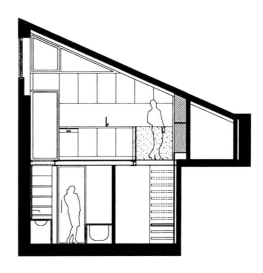

Section A

Lobina House

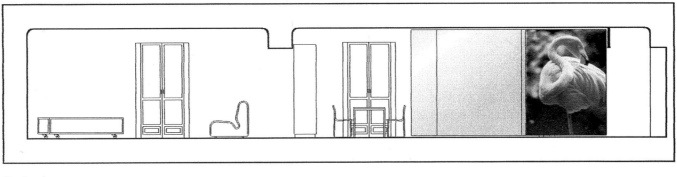

Section A

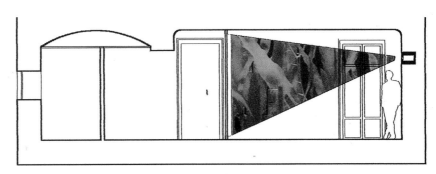

Section B

Floor plan

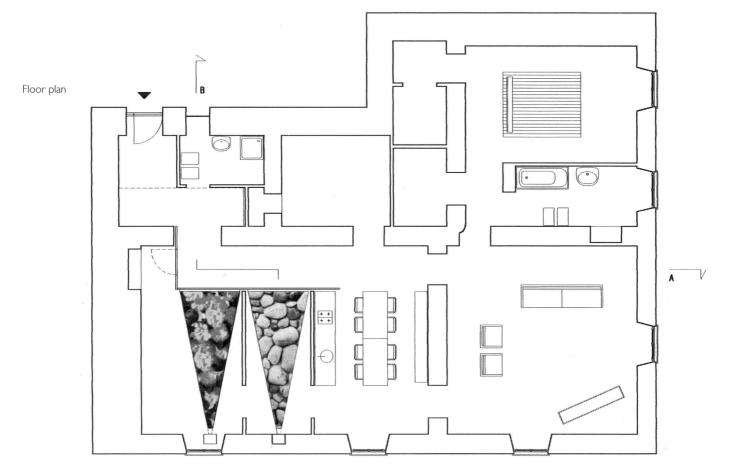

Wiel Arets
Home Office of the Architect

Maastricht, The Netherlands

An interpretation of the specific restrictions on the site imposed by various building regulations dictated a maximum volumetric envelope.

It is into this simple volume that the complex and diverse home and office program was installed.

The confrontation between the restrictions of the site and the complexity of the brief framed the subsequent architectural manipulations. Set on a sloping corner allotment in a suburban housing and villa area on the edge of the historic center of Maastricht, the disparity between the simplicity of its appearance and the complex spatial arrangement of the interior accentuates the perverse qualities of suburban life splendidly explored by David Lynch's "Blue Velvet".

The building uses the natural slope of the site to articulate a section that allows one to enter the house from street level to an interior mezzanine before descending to the garden level or rising to the third level. The building is divided vertically by a technical space, cocooned in turn by a diaphragm party wall into the two functionally different areas of the office and the home. The sectional deviation allows the building to maximize its prescribed envelope of 1.5 stories above and 1.5 stories below street level and to increase inter-floor communication.

A concrete box is embedded into the site with primary views through large openings to the garden and courtyard; the second more private wooden box is set on top, fronting onto the street and the garden behind.

The top level within the wooden box contains the bedrooms and the meeting room, administration and director's office. One descends to the 'ground floor', which contains the living areas and the kitchen and opens onto the expansive garden, swimming pool and terrace. The 'ground floor' office space and project room opens to the side facing away from the private garden to a walled courtyard with glass brick floor. The lower level is for the office. It extends below the house and contains the drawing room, archive, workshop and preparation areas. Light enters through the glass bricks of the walled courtyard and through windows that open onto areas of the garden that are scalloped out and shielded from the inhabitants of the house section.

Photographs: Kim Zwarts

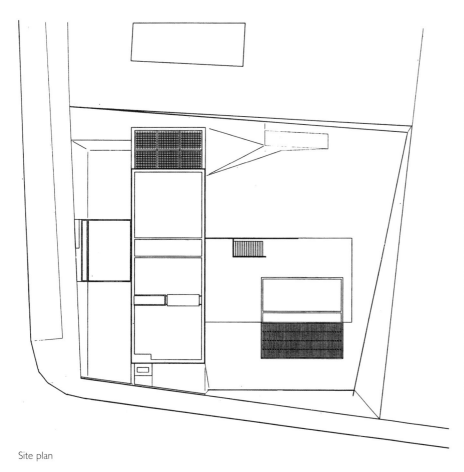

Site plan

Basement floor plan

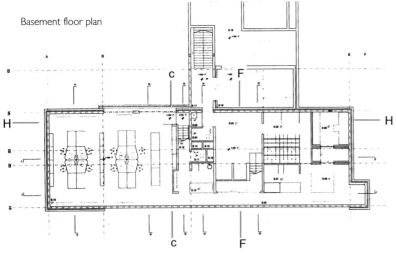

Ground floor plan

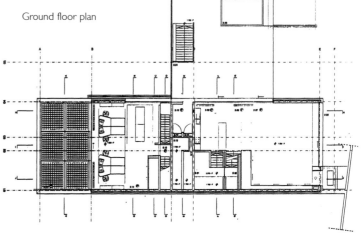

First floor plan

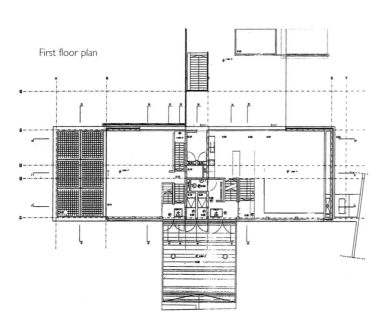

Second floor plan

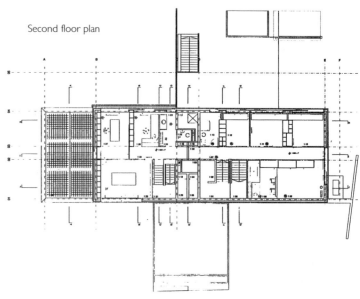

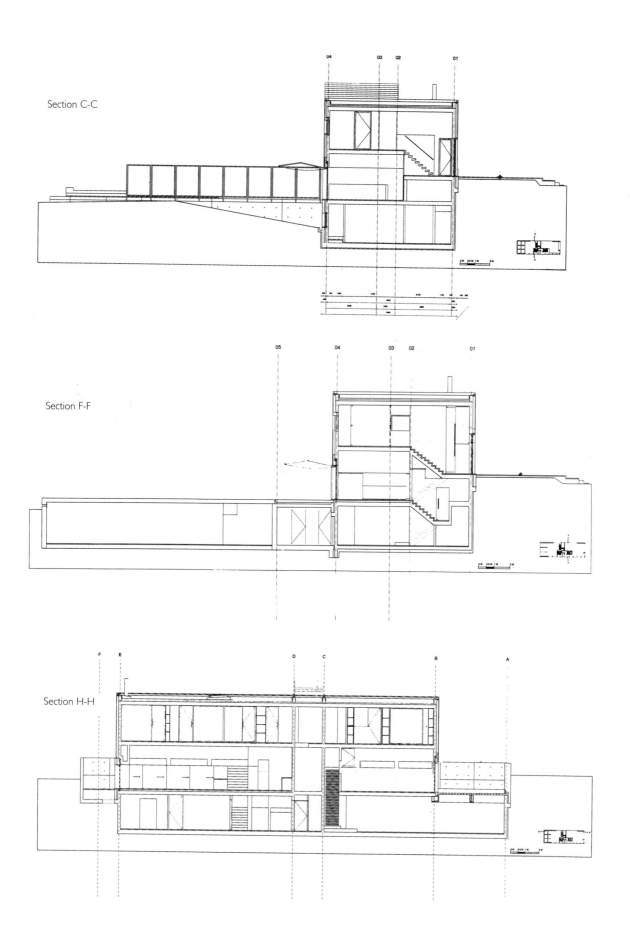

Section C-C

Section F-F

Section H-H

The extremely simple appearance of the exterior contrasts with the complex spatial distribution of the interior. The building is divided vertically by a nucleus of installations that separates a plan that includes an office and a dwelling.

The exterior of the building is structured as a concrete box with large glazed openings that offer views onto the garden and the courtyard. On this concrete nucleus a more private wooden box is deposited, with openings to the street and rear garden.

ARCHITECTUS:
Bowes, Clifford + Thompson
Private Residence Auckland

Auckland, New Zealand

This elegant house, by the Auckland firm Architectus, comes as a surprise in its suburban setting, which is an intimate valley formed by a stream flowing into a tidal basin. Its architectural context is a pleasantly anarchic collection of houses on steep slopes leading down to the water. The site is a leftover triangle of land above the stream, reached from a shared drive. In this ad hoc context, typical of Auckland's hilly suburbs, the architects have inserted a highly ordered pavilion, which responds inventively to its site.
The formality, the simple, strong geometric basis, structural clarity and even the combination of simple unadorned materials (concrete block, timber and glass) recall Kahn. But while Kahn usually avoided overall symmetry in his houses, Architectus delight in the balanced purity of this structure. Purity is more than visual formalism: it conceals great density of use, privacy, view and climate.
The house is planned on a 3940 ft^2 module on three levels: the middle entry floor has living areas, with bedroom floor above and space for visitors below. Due to the restricted site area, privacy problems from houses to the east and west, and the need for protection from the western sun, the interior opens south and north (to make use of the northern light predominating in the southern hemisphere) along the valley, providing the living area with views through trees and toward the tidal basin. An intimate semi-enclosed deck between the building and hillside is created as the entry court and morning terrace.
The building is rigorously laid out in three layers running roughly north-south along the contours: a service zone for kitchen, bathrooms and circulation, a wider central zone for principal served spaces, and two projecting bays on upper levels that expand the living spaces and become voids at bedroom level. The plan is symmetrically organized around its east-west axis, with an a-b-a-b structural bay rhythm. On the middle level, living space is extended with cantilevered decks at each end: the central bay denotes entry, while the two wider bays accommodate dining area/kitchen and sitting area/staircase respectively. On the upper level, the tripartite division of the served space becomes two bedrooms separated by a dressing room.
So the main rooms of the house, though visually or physically opening out into other spaces vertically and horizontally, are identified as 39 ft^2 bays, elegantly framed by slender laminated timber posts. In winter, the east-west axes of the living spaces are emphasized, extending into the projecting bays, while in summer, with folding doors open at both ends (solid to living and glazed to dining), the space becomes linear, extending out north and south into the landscape.

Photographs: Patrick Reynolds, Paul McCreadie

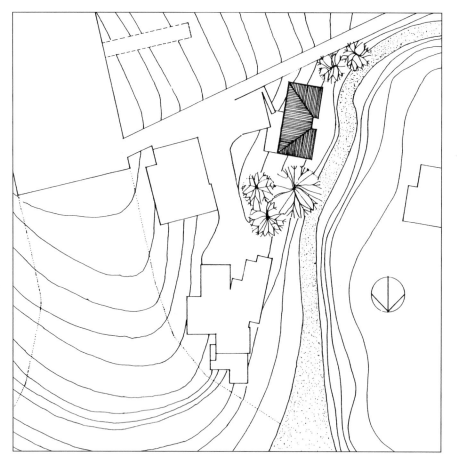

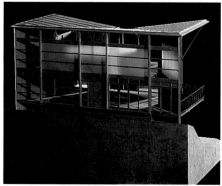

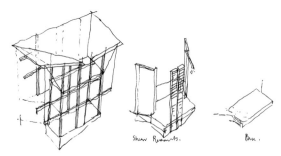

The primary elements of construction, frame and walls, are given a concrete base to sit on, which is mostly used as a covered terrace, and the whole topped by a folded plate roof, underlined with plywood.

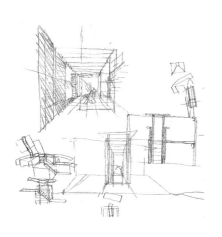

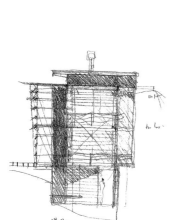

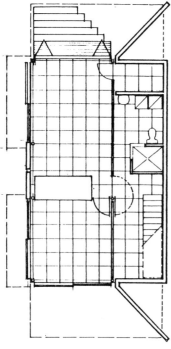

First floor plan

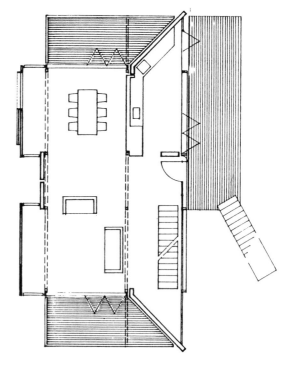

Second floor plan

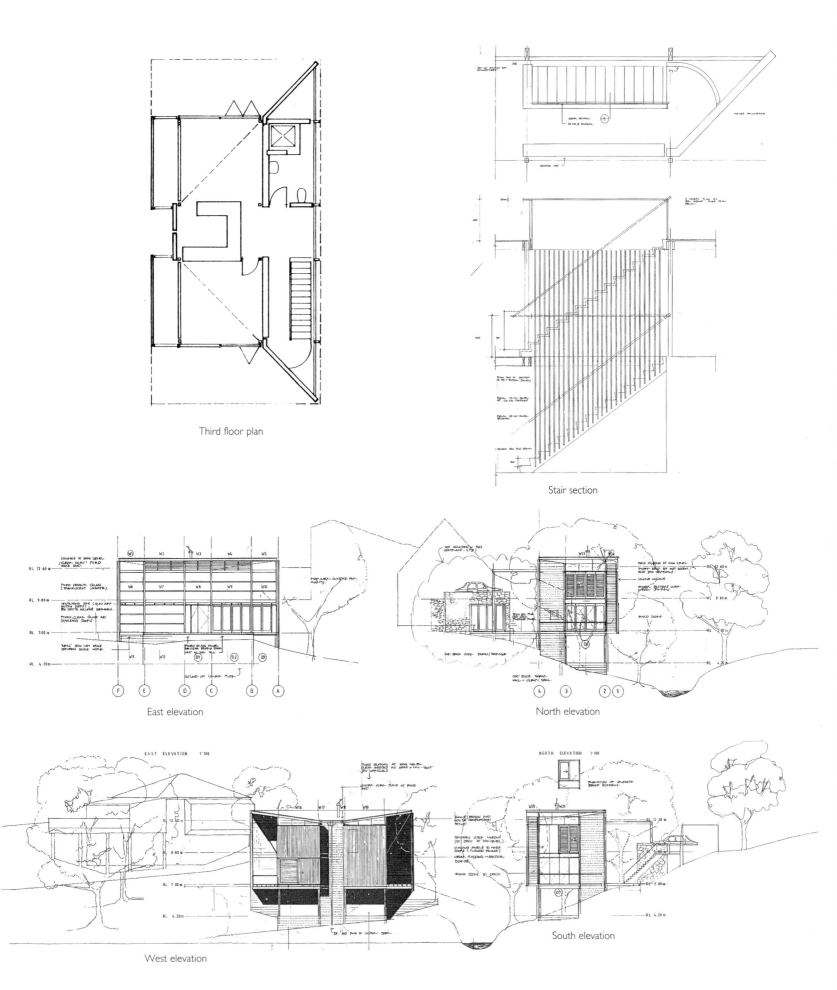

Third floor plan

Stair section

East elevation

North elevation

West elevation

South elevation

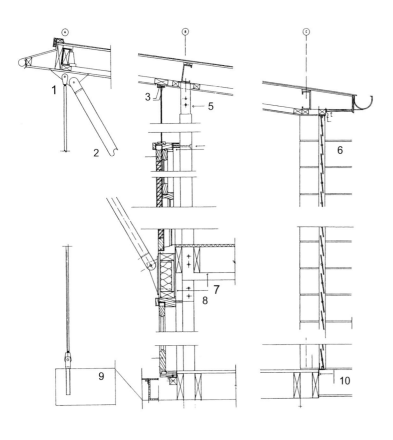

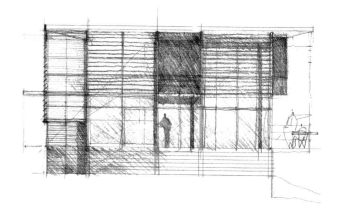

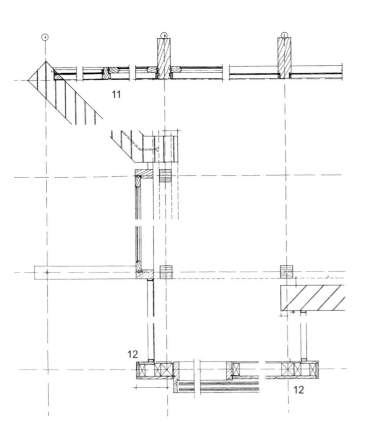

1. MS bracket, forked ends to the rod and strut,
   12mm shear pin with clip connector
2. 70mm compression strut
3. Timber glazing beads
4. Typical column head detail
5. Sliding-folding screens
6. Block work shown in elevation beyond
7. Stringer
8. Plywood lining
9. Steel balcony
10. Aluminum support angle
11. 20×10 glazing bead
12. Shiplap boards

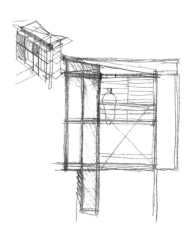

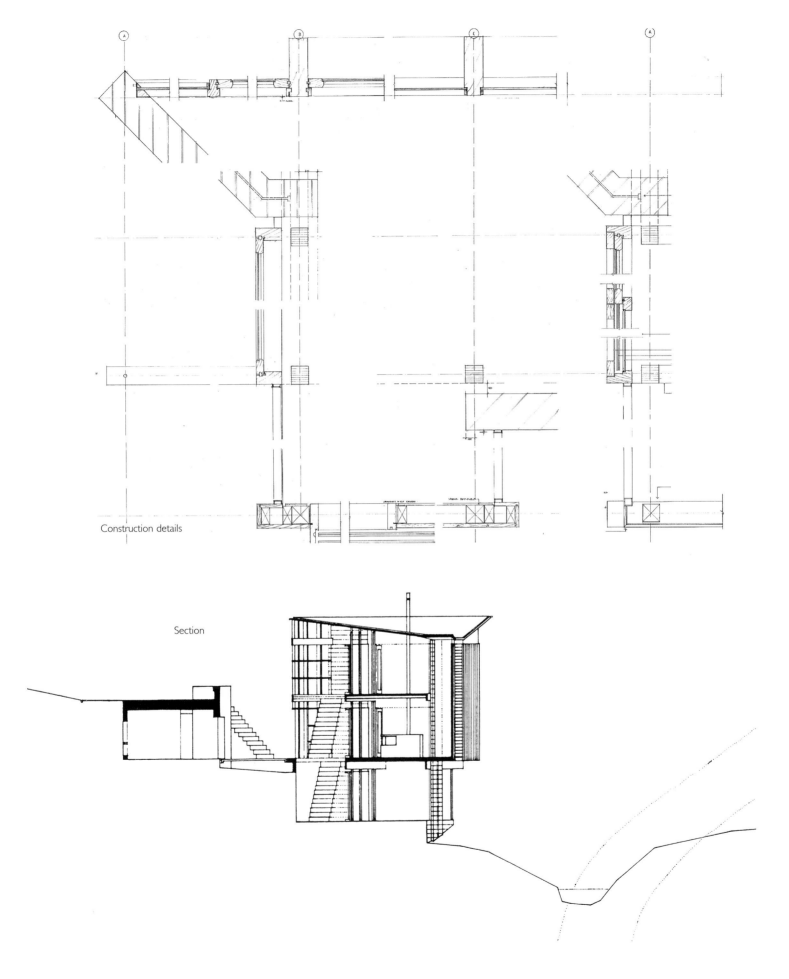

Construction details

Section

Bürlingschindler Freie Architekten BDA
House in Albbruck

Albbruck, Germany

This project in Albbruck called for the construction of a home for a family with children. The building conforms to the slope of the south wing of the plot and the entrance is gained by a private path. One of the aims of this program was to design a home which would be flexible enough to cope with the changing needs of its inhabitants; in short, a structure with the ability to adapt to their growth, their lives, the seasons and different times of day. It therefore had to follow a flexible, easily modifiable plan.

A three-part program was adopted. A module with a double-sloping roof was erected parallel to the eastern zone of the dwelling and contains the dining room, sitting room and kitchen. In the western portion, an annex is joined to the main part of the building through a glazed corridor. To the south, a terrace of wood planks allows the owners to move their activities outdoors when fair weather allows. The difference in height between the various modules and the large quantity of glass panels throughout the building facilitate the entrance of abundant natural light in this home.

This program displays a compact yet spacious design, which seeks to connect the various spaces without sacrificing privacy. The more public areas open onto the terraces to the south and west. The glazed corridor is a transition zone which joins the annex and the building's main volume, and which can be used as a cloakroom, although other uses can be assigned to the space. The flexibility of the vertical faces makes this space easily adaptable to different occasions: parties, meetings and so forth. The northern portion contains a staircase, bathroom, toilet, a maid's bedroom and a utility room. A wide corridor, which also serves as a play area, leads to the master bedroom and the children's bedrooms. The annex module consists of a single story, which houses a guest bedroom that can double as a studio. A sauna or a bar for social gatherings can also be installed in this same space. The northern portion is a two-storey volume. The upper floor is an especially flexible and unique space with spaces for various uses: a work area, a playroom, a guest bedroom and so forth. Large south-facing windows let in plenty of natural light here. A second bathroom is located next to the staircase.

Photographs: Andreas Keller

Site plan

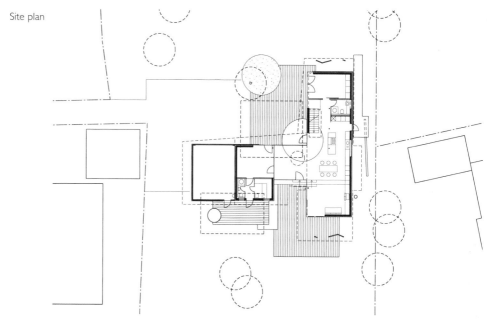

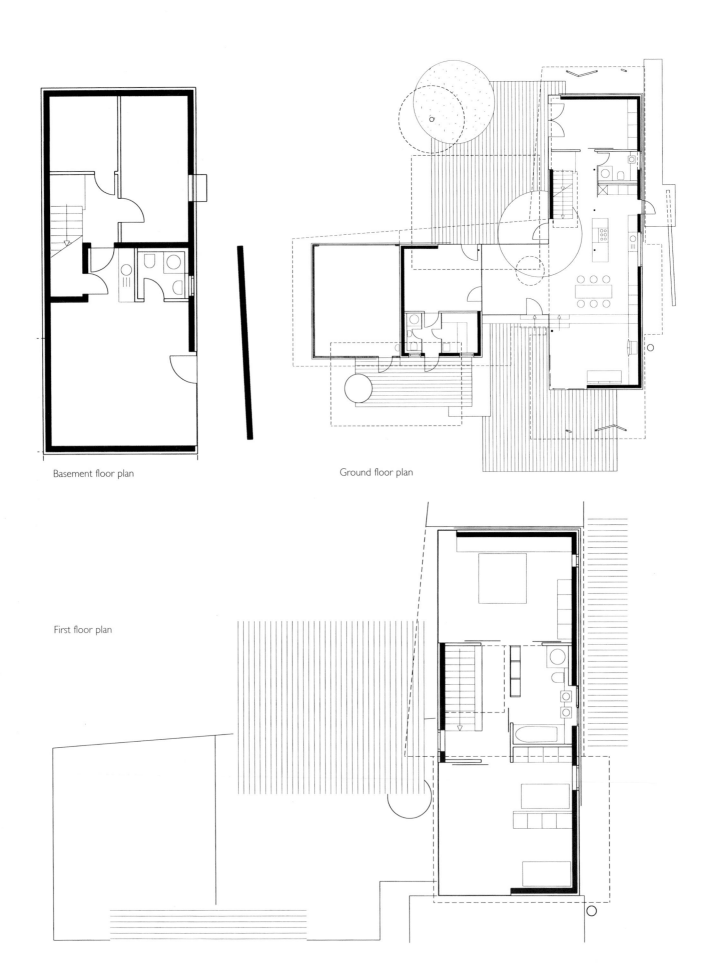

Basement floor plan

Ground floor plan

First floor plan

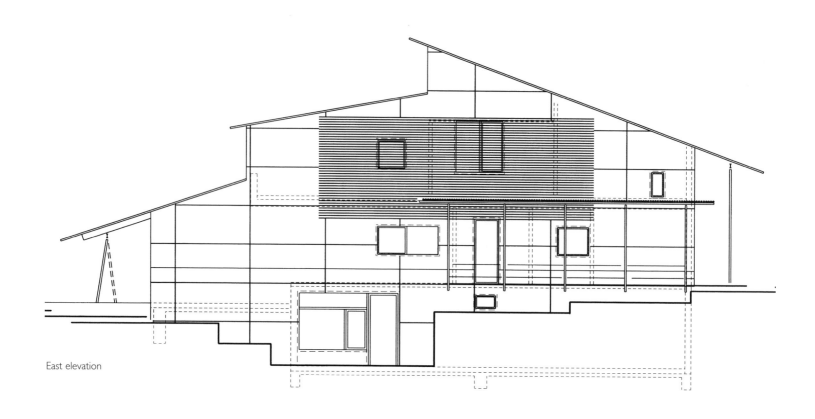

East elevation

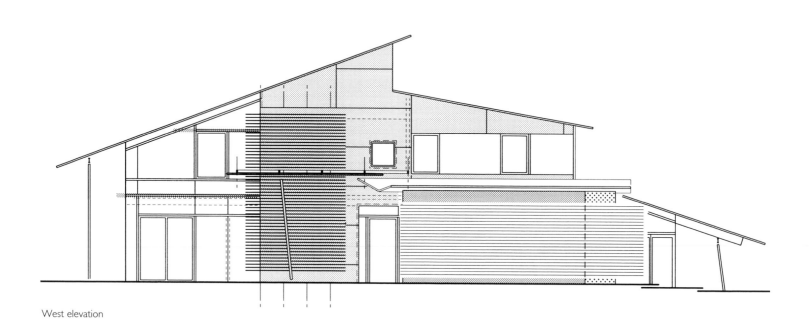

West elevation

The unevenness of the roof fills the dwelling with abundant light. A terrace, accessed from the living room, has been added to the south side of the building.

The aim of this project is to conjoin the dwelling's different spaces, using stairs to link the various rooms. The kitchen, located on the lower floor, is connected to the rest of the home by a few steps, which lead to the first floor.

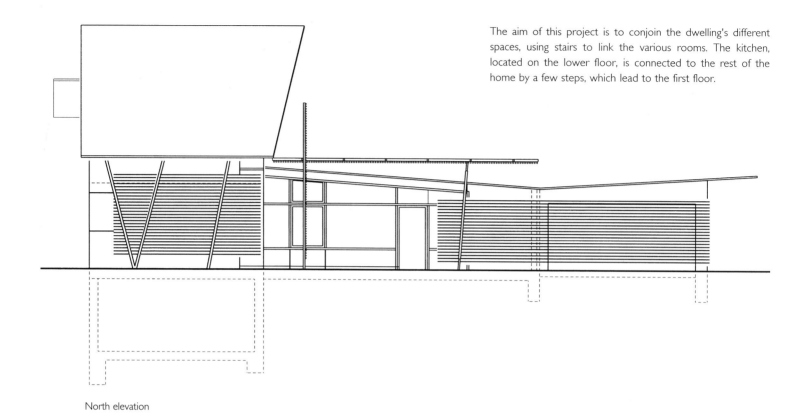

North elevation

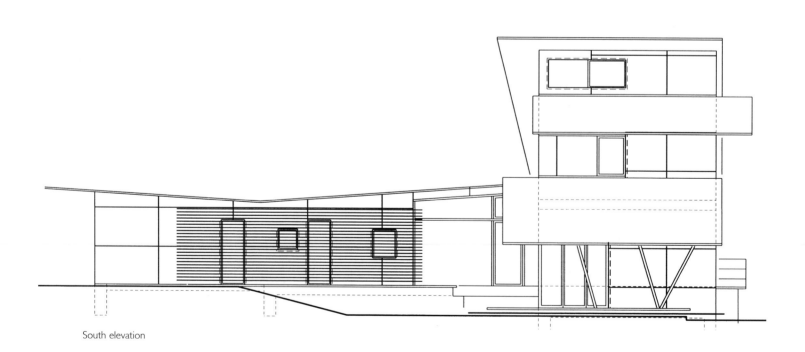

South elevation

On the first floor, a large, spacious volume which
houses the day-use areas opens onto the yard,
which is partially clad in wood and has a pool.

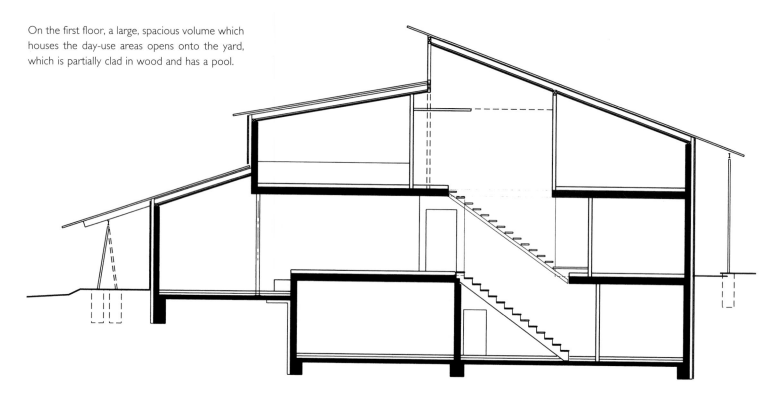

Sections

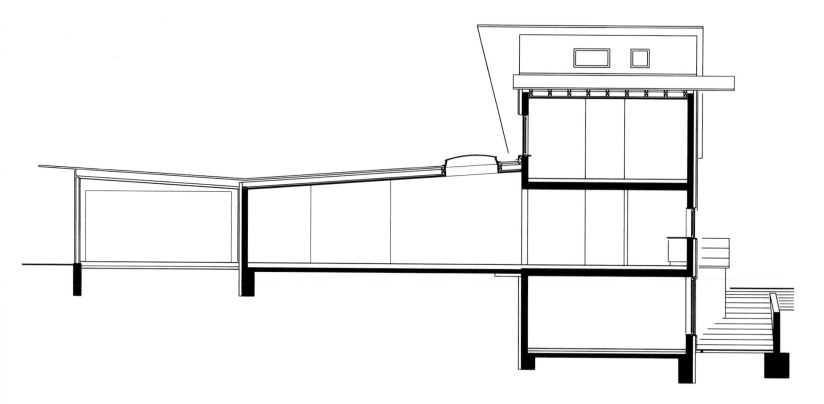

Anthony Hudson & Sarah Featherstone
Voss Street House

London, UK

A mixed use development on a site comprising a shop facing onto Bethnal Green Road, a self-contained studio and a two-bedroom house above. The architect (also the home's owner) had to address two primary concerns in the design: the need for privacy from the busy commercial street and overcoming the serious spatial limitations presented by a plot which was only 4m wide.

The site's spatial restrictions were resolved by the creation of high-ceilinged, diaphanous spaces, entirely free of connecting corridors. Instead, a lozenge-shaped spiral staircase was built - most of its volume jutting out into the central courtyard- providing access to each individual level.

Privacy, as well as abundant natural light, have been achieved by arranging the rooms around the central courtyard, with all windows facing inward. There are no windows in the south-facing elevation; while the only window on the north facade has been fitted with etched glass in order to filter light in while blocking views of the street outside.

The house is a retreat which turns its back on the street, while also providing a generosity of light, space and materiality within the constraints of an awkward site.

Photographs: Tim Brotherton

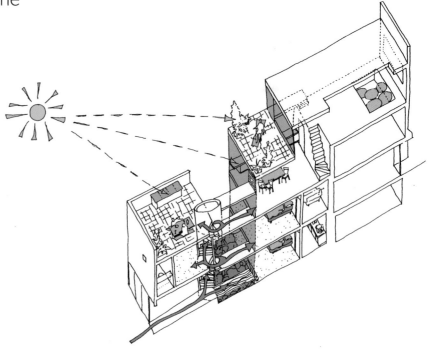

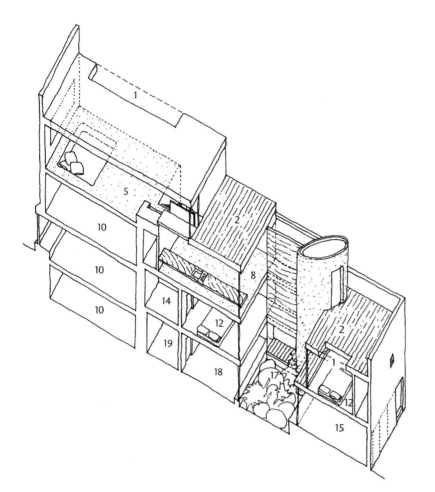

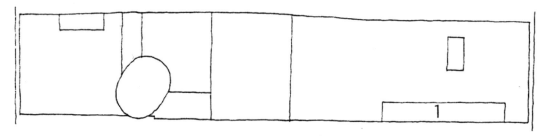

Roof plan

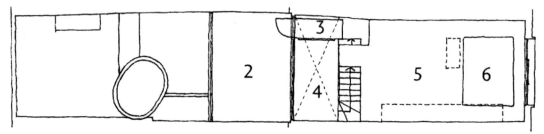

Second-third floor plan

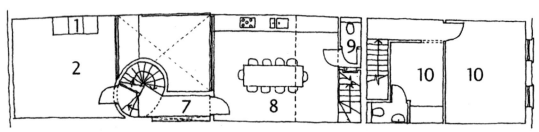

First-second floor plan

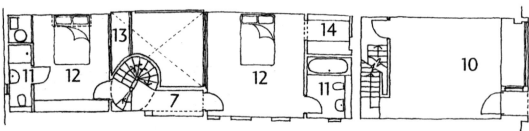

Upper ground-first floor plan

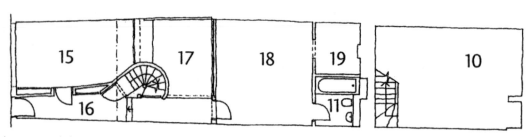

Lower ground plan

1. Rooflight
2. Roof terrace
3. Bridge
4. Double-height void
5. Living room
6. Conversation pit
7. Landing
8. Kitchen-dining
9. WC
10. Retail unit
11. Bathroom
12. Bedroom
13. Balcony
14. Dressing room
15. Garage-store
16. Entrance hall
17. Courtyard
18. Studio
19. Utility room

To ensure privacy and bring more light into the building, the rooms are arranged around a central courtyard, stacked one above the other at staggered half levels, all looking inwards.

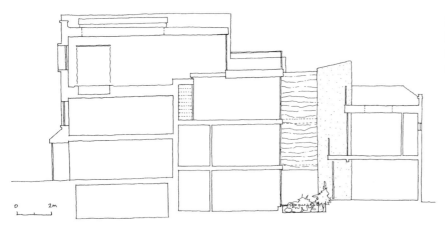

Because of the small scale, there was no room for corridors; hence, the creation of a spiral stairwell, as seen in the axonometric projection below. This entirely enclosed structure juts out into the courtyard and provides access to each separate level.

Longitudinal section

Wolfgang Feyferlik & Susanne Fritzer
Cortolezis House

Graz, Austria

This project consisted of the construction of a home on a sloped plot for a family with three children. Two different roads lead from the urban center to the house, which was built on the lower part of the plot. The main volume, supported by pillars, was erected one floor above the ground, thus freeing up the space below for use as a covered passage.

The main entrance, entirely glazed, is also located in this "foyer". The master bedroom, kitchen, dining room and sitting room, as well as the wood terrace and swimming pool are situated in the center of the dwelling on the upper portion of the plot. The children's bedrooms lie below the west end of the terrace in a separate module, which is partially underground. These modules could be entirely separated from the main bulk of the residence, as if they were individual pieces. The materials used for the construction of this dwelling were basically concrete for the master walls and garden walls and a 7mm thick plastic material for the facades and glazed walls.

The garden areas located in front of the building can be used independently, without establishing any visual contact between them.

Photographs: Ralph Richter/Architekturphoto

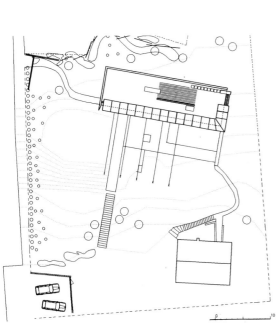

Site plan

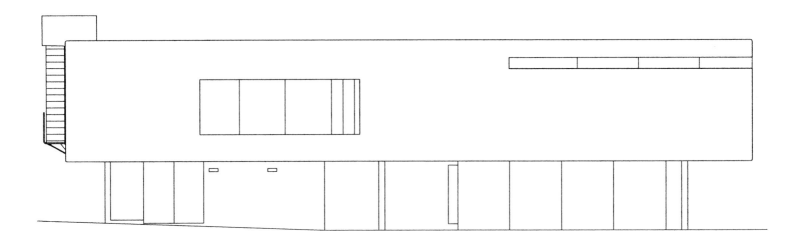

North elevation

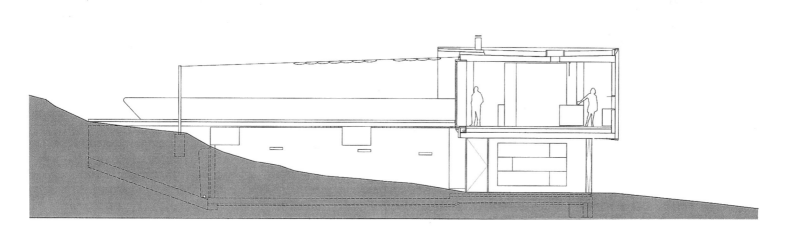

Section

An open staircase in front of the eastern glazed facade leads to the roof, which doubles as a terrace and from which bathers can jump directly into the pool.

Main floor plan

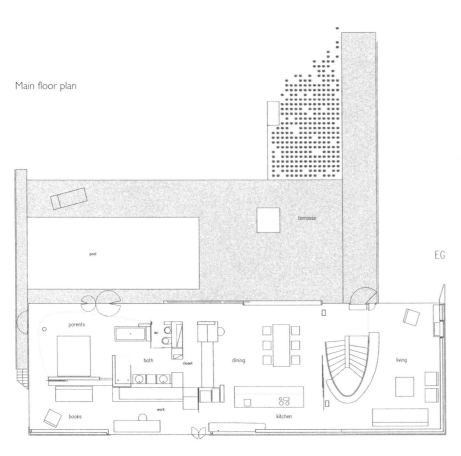

pool

terrasse

EG

parents

wc

bath   closet   dining   living

books   work   kitchen

Rataplan
Studio Flat

Wien, Austria

An entire floor of a former archive in Vienna from the turn of the century was opened up to create a new studio flat. In the original plan only a glass-covered hall illuminated the floor, but a large window now serves as a source of light, creating visual links with the outside world and providing a means of ventilation.

The 4.75-meter-high space is divided by two steel wall slabs that help retain the industrial character of the building and the aesthetics and volume of the hall area. Parallel to these are smaller red panels. This layering effect marks the thresholds to the more intimate zones. The rooms are closed off with full-height sheets of glass, which facilitate visual contact both internally and externally and maintain the relationship of the rooms with the hall and with the exterior. The space thus gains a new variety of heights and surfaces, new perspectives, lighting, intimacy and openness. The contrast between cool steel, the warm surfaces of the wood floor and the bold red of the wall panels reflects the use of the object as a studio and dwelling.

Photographs: Markus Tomaselli

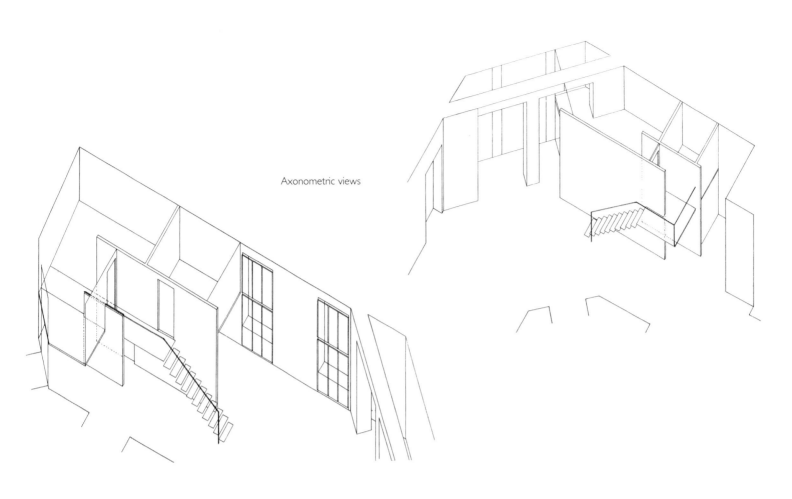

Axonometric views

Upper level floor plan

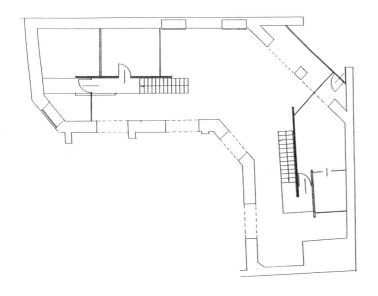

Lower level floor plan

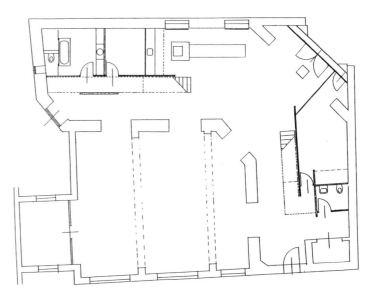

Plan of the access to the upper floor plan

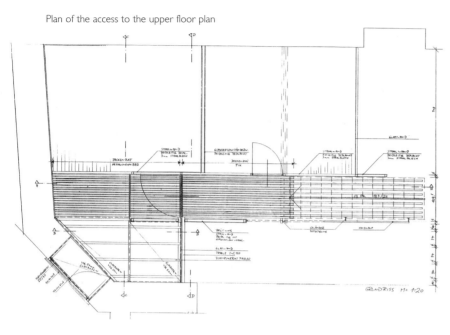

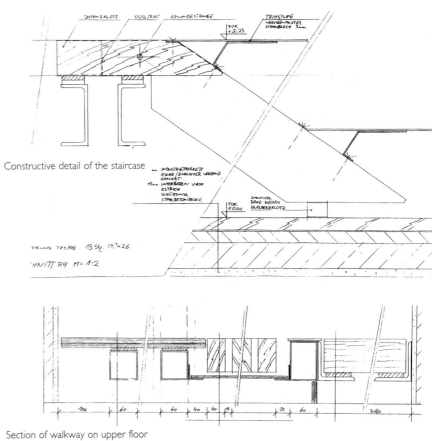

Constructive detail of the staircase

Section of walkway on upper floor

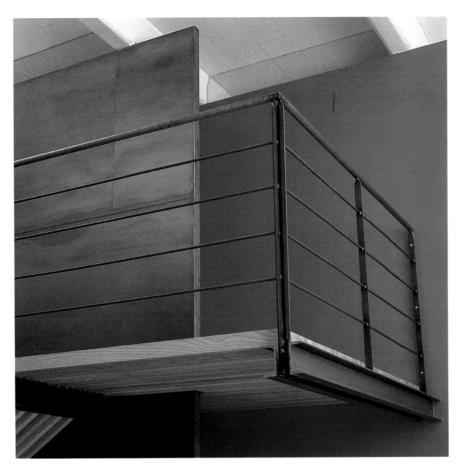

The rooms have been closed off with full-height glass panels. The interior organization of the dwelling is structured on the basis of two staircases supported by walls clad with metal plates.

Fraser Brown MacKenna
Derbyshire St. Residence

London, UK

Following personal recommendations, Fraser Brown MacKenna Architects were chosen by the client to restore the two upper floors of a converted loft in Bethnal Green. A dramatic barrel vaulted Perspex roof had been added to the building but spaces within were subdivided and darked.

A translucent floor was used in a double-height space, the upper floor being used as the main area with the kitchen and dining room. The lower floor was stripped and opened to achieve a large flexible level for sleeping, working and living. On this floor, a ten meter long, full height Plexiglas screen, divides storage and utility spaces from the main circulation and living areas in the building. It provides a bright, clean plane in contrast to the large expanse of the restored floorboards. The light is reflected in it, causing effects of brightness and shade that give the impression that the light comes alive as one moves. This screen can be manipulated to modify the space, thus creating a new area for sleeping, talking or relaxing and allowing the space to adapt to the needs of the owners. The screen employs a bold language, expressed in the stainless steel socket cap head screws and aluminum T-sections. Against the screen, the simple geometry of the copper cladding of the storage area reveals within its natural patina a hundred hues to play against the subtle shadows of light. The simple form of screen, box, sink and fin walls formed from glass blocks or perforated metal acknowledges the space and what it had previously been.

Photographs: Nick Hufton

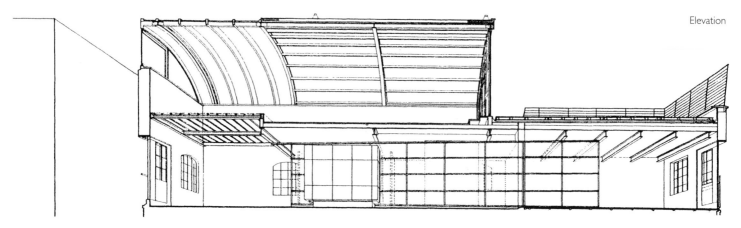

Elevation

Elevation

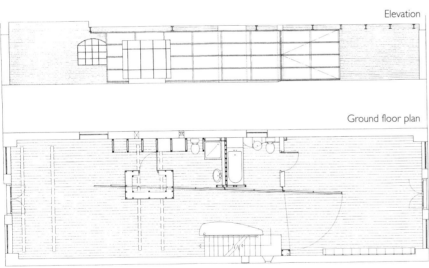

Ground floor plan

First floor plan

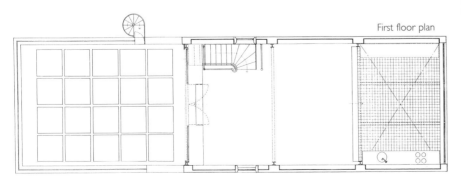

A Plexiglas screen divides and modifies the space according to the needs of its owners. The material gives a modern touch and the light filtering through it illuminates the whole apartment.

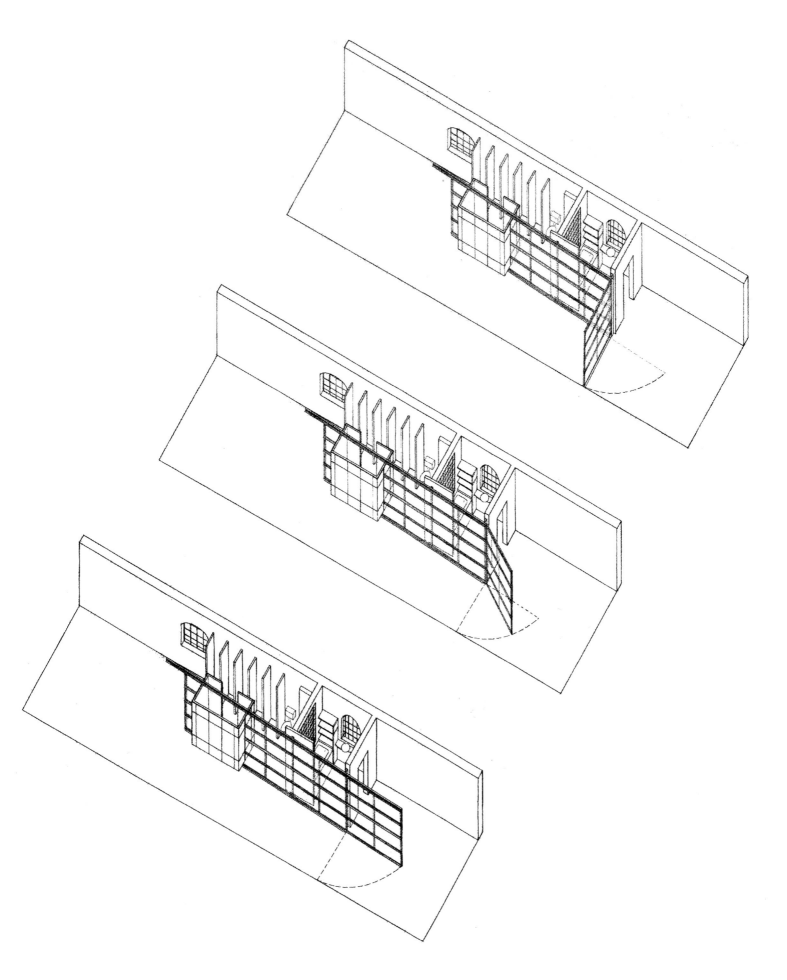

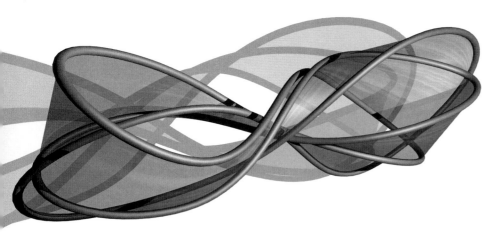

Un Studio Van Berkel & Bos
Möbius House

Het Gooi, The Netherlands

The diagram of the double-locked torus conveys the organization of two intertwining paths, which trace how two people can live together, yet apart, meeting at certain points, which become shared spaces. The idea of two entities running their own trajectories but sharing certain moments, possibly also reversing roles at certain points, is extended to include the materialization of the building and its construction.

The Möbius house integrates program, circulation and structure seamlessly. The house interweaves the various states that accompany the condensation of differentiating activities into one structure: work, social life, family life and individual time alone all find their places in the loop structure. Movement through this loop follows the pattern of an active day. The structure of movement is transposed to the organization of the two main materials used for the house; glass and concrete move in front of each other and switch places. Concrete construction becomes furniture and glass facades turn into inside partition walls.

As a graphic representation of 24 hours of family life, the diagram acquires a time-space dimension, which leads to the implementation of the Möbius band. Equally the site and its relationship to the building are important for the design. The site covers two hectares, which are divided into four distinct areas. Linking these with the internal organization of the Möbius band transforms living in the house into a walk in the landscape.

The mathematical model of the Möbius is not literally transferred to the building, but is conceptualized and can be found in architectural ingredients, such as the light, the staircases and the way in which people move through the house. So, while the Möbius diagram introduces aspects of duration and trajectory, the diagram is worked into the building in a mutated way.

The instrumentalization of this simple drawing is the key. The two interlocking lines are suggestive of the formal organization of the building, but that is only the beginning; diagrammatic architecture is a process of unfolding and ultimately of liberation. The diagram liberates architecture from language, interpretation and signification.

Photographs: Christian Richters

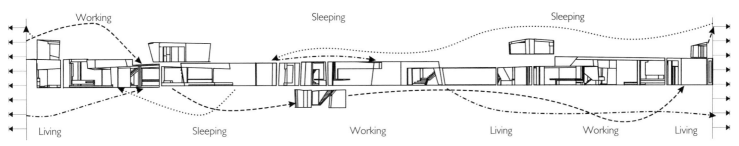

Working   Sleeping   Sleeping

Living   Sleeping   Working   Living   Working   Living

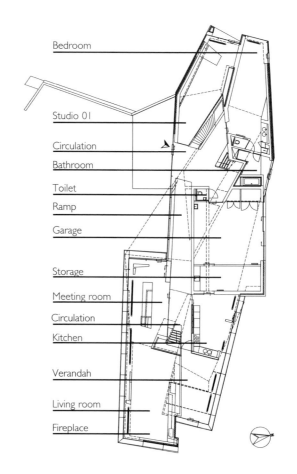

Bedroom

Studio 01

Circulation

Bathroom

Toilet

Ramp

Garage

Storage

Meeting room

Circulation

Kitchen

Verandah

Living room

Fireplace

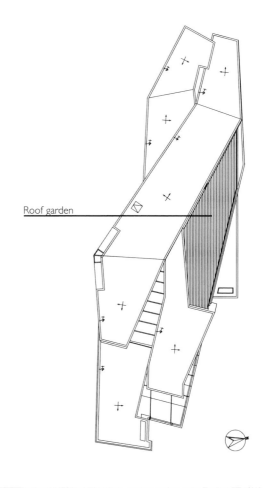

Roof garden

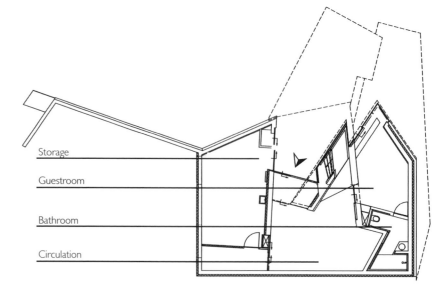

Storage

Guestroom

Bathroom

Circulation

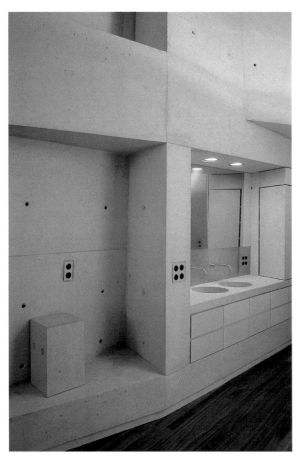

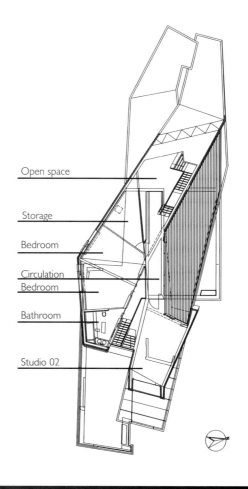

Open space

Storage

Bedroom

Circulation
Bedroom

Bathroom

Studio 02

Richard Rogers Partnership
House in Royal Avenue

London, UK

For their own dwelling, Richard and Ruth Rogers renovated two five-story terrace houses built in 1840 on Royal Avenue. They are on a corner site overlooking Wren's beautiful 1692 Royal Hospital and the King's Road. Both properties are Grade II historic building and had small dark gardens to the rear which were devoid of sunlight due to the encroachment of the surrounding buildings.

Functionally, the house is divided horizontally. The older children and nanny live in three flats in the basement. Ruth's mother has the ground floor. Richard and Ruth live primarily on the second and third floors and the younger children and study are on the fourth floor.

The original dark courtyard at the back is glazed over to form a three-story-high entry hall and playroom area. A spiral staircase connects all five floors and bypasses the principle living and mezzanine sleeping areas.

A small garden terrace runs off the side of the kitchen area. The party wall between the two houses was replaced by a steel structure on the second, third and fourth floors. The second floor was partially removed and replaced and a mezzanine was formed creating a magnificent double height space at first-floor level of approximately 7 meters in height. This provided the main living area with the kitchen at first-floor level and the bedroom and bathroom on the mezzanine. The kitchen with its stainless steel island is a central feature of the space.

Photographs: Richard Bryant / Arcaid

The interior is organized as a single, continuous space in which the various functional activities take place.
Here, views of the master bedroom located on the upper floor and the final flight of the agile and translucent metal staircase.

Rem Koolhaas
Dutch House

The Netherlands

The 5000 m² site is located in a forest of pine on fine golden beach sand. Aside from the unstable ground conditions, specific site requirements included a height restriction of four meters above the adjacent road and an excessive limitation of buildable area. Literal interpretations of these givens dictated the maximum frame; manipulations of the terrain were subsequent. A drive-through path was carved out to ensure efficiency of access and exit.

The program consists of facilities for two permanent residents and their three grown-up daughters, who visit occasionally. To fade the presence of their absence, a programmatic split was introduced, materialized by the slab —held by one house, holding the other. The focus of the architects was on how to translate two different conditions of occupation related to specific site conditions as autonomous elements with moments of interaction, and further, how to compress a maximum program into a minimum of formal gestures.

At ground level, one wrapping wall defines a continuity of interior spaces and patios for the daughters' quarters, which is an introverted and grounded space.

The floating deck supports a crystallized container of the parents' program. A single hinge —the pivoting bridge/horizontal door— feeds both bedroom units with patio above, service entry below. The wall itself contains all functional elements, dictating adjacent activity but leaving the surrounding space free within the glass box, which is physically detached from but visually inclusive of the surrounding landscape.

The node of the house is a central ramp providing visual and functional connection between the two counterparts.

Photographs: Christian Richters

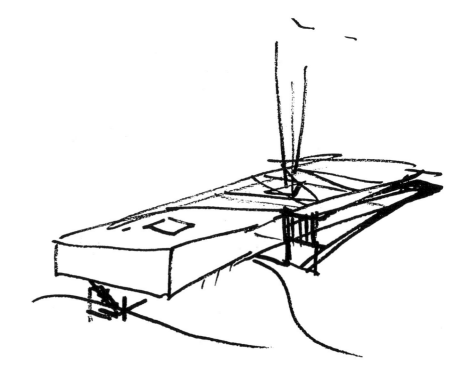

Cross-sections through the access ramp

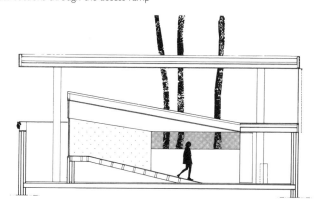 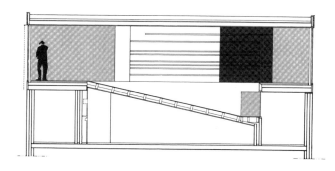

Upper floor plan

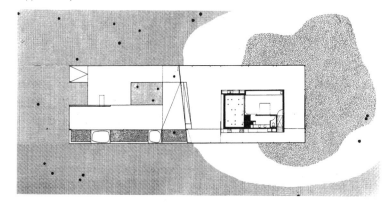

Lower floor plan

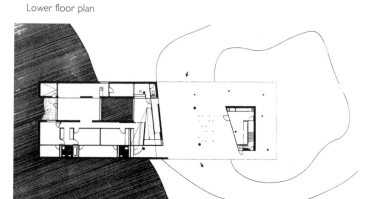

Araceli Manzano & Esther Flavià
House in Argentona

Argentona, Spain

This dwelling, located on a particularly long rectangular plot (5x22 m), maintains the structure of the houses that are typical in the area: ground floor with direct access from the street, first floor and a small court at the rear. The intervention aimed to respect the existing structure as far as possible, but due to its extremely deteriorated state it was only possible to conserve the stone party walls, the front facade and the wooden structure.

The roofing bricks and a wooden beam structure had been concealed behind a vaulted drop ceiling, which had to be demolished. The wooden structure of the roof was repaired and the tiles were replaced, over a layer of insulation. Removing the drop ceiling increased the height of the first floor, making it possible to build a mezzanine, formed by a light metal structure covered with wooden boards.

The original front facade was conserved, although the woodwork had to be replaced, and wooden shutters were added. The rear facade was modified to increase the size of the openings and obtain better lighting. A sizeable landscaped courtyard was created by the demolition of the small buildings adjacent to the house.

On the ground floor the kitchen was located on the facade, so it became a particularly attractive element due to its situation on the street and the amount of daylight that it receives. The rest of the floor is a large living/dining room that opens onto the court through a large wooden window. A system of sliding doors was used between the living room, the kitchen and the access, thus creating an extremely fluid relation between the rooms.

On the first floor, two double rooms with dressing room and bathroom, situated symmetrically in relation to the floor plan, use the front and rear facades to ventilate directly to the street. The totally open floor plan of the mezzanine was created for use as an office or gym, but could easily be converted into two independent rooms. The location of the rooms on the facade leaves free the central space, where double-height spaces not coinciding in the whole height are used to develop the stairs. The treatment of the double spaces tempers the view of the real height of the house from all the floors.

Photographs: Eugeni Pons

348

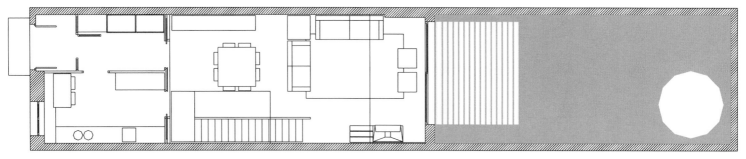

Ground floor plan

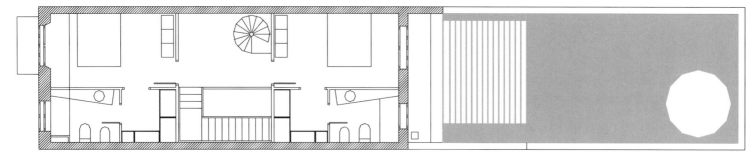

First floor plan

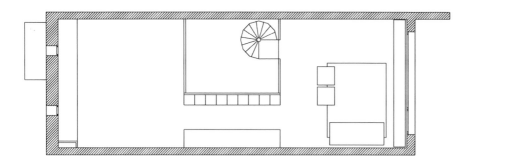

Roof floor plan

0   5

The floor cladding is of waxed chestnut floorboards; the long side wall of the living room was painted with iron oxide, and all the wooden elements (wardrobes, banisters, door frames) with colored enamel in order to highlight the volumetrics.

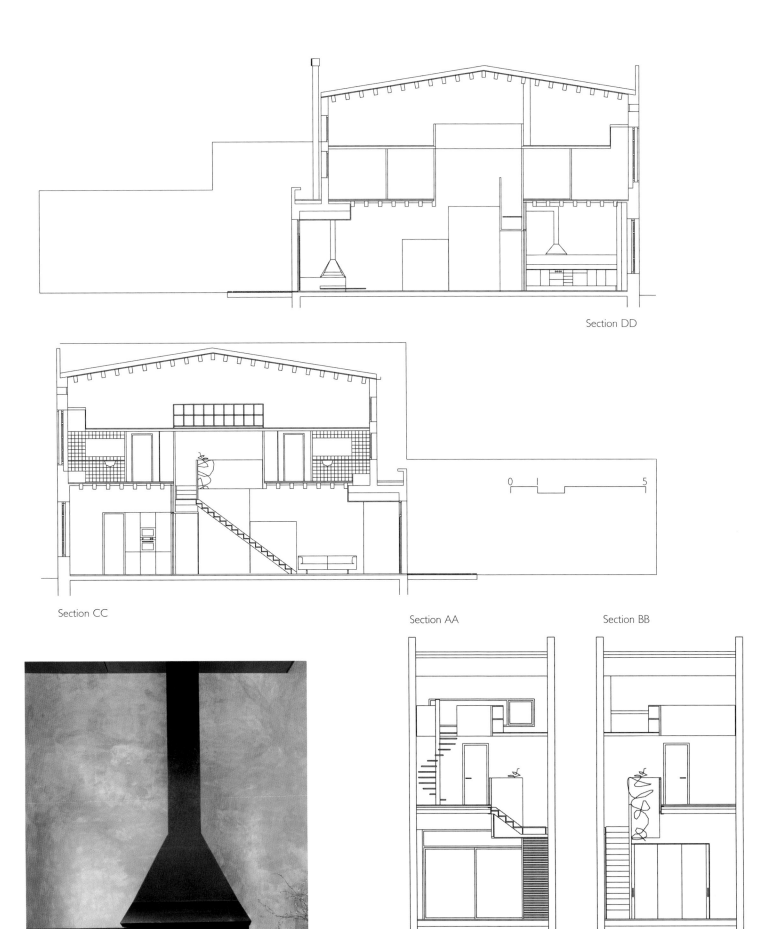

Section DD

Section CC

Section AA

Section BB

0 | | | | | 5

On the first floor, two double rooms with dressing room and bathroom, situated symmetrically in relation to the floor plan, use the front and rear facades for ventilation.

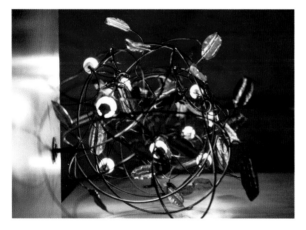

Robert M. Gurney
Fitch/O'Rourke Residence

Washington DC, USA

A thorough renovation converted this townhouse, for years the neighborhood eyesore, into a modern, warm, and intimate residence with light-filled two- and three-story spaces and a mix of rich and unexpected materials.

The owner's program included a two-bedroom, two-study residence (convertible into three bedrooms and one study) on the upper three levels, and a one-bedroom rental unit in the basement. The project faced two serious constraints. On the one hand was the house's long, narrow footprint (63 feet long, about 17 feet wide on the front, narrowing to 13 feet), which traditionally had dictated an in-line room arrangement; and on the other was the property's location in a designated historic district, which required the front facade to be kept intact.

The renovation, which began with two brick side walls and a basement dirt floor, amounted to building a new house inside an old shell. The design for the project transcends the building's narrow confines by combining a traditional orthogonal scheme with a curving geometry (where most curves and radials trace back to a center point 28 feet east of the house) and a rotation space (based on a ten degree diagonal running from a rear corner to the center of the dining room).

The living room exploits the southern exposure and the opportunity to build a new rear facade that could bring light into a lofted space. A second lofted area near the front brings light into the northern end.

A wide range of materials was chosen to create a rich and warm mix of colors and textures and to admit and modulate light. They include concrete, steel (force-rusted, stainless, perforated, painted), block aluminum, lead-coated copper, copper wire cloth, Uniclad corrugated panels, clear and sandblasted glass, limestone tile, maple and mahogany veneer cabinets and wall panels, and Kalwall and Lumicite translucent panels.

Photographs: Paul Warchol & Anice Hoachlander

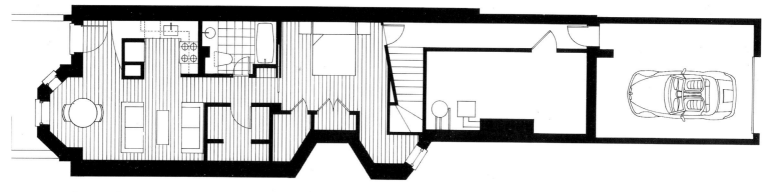

Basement floor plan

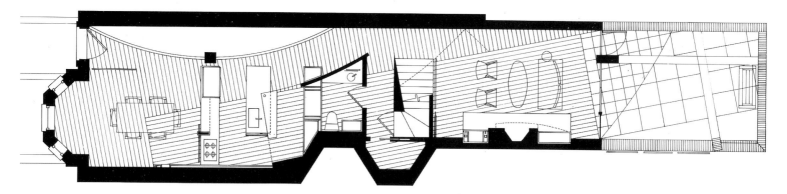

First floor plan

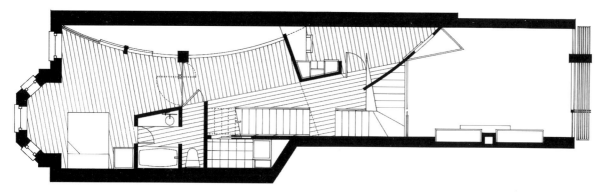

Second floor plan

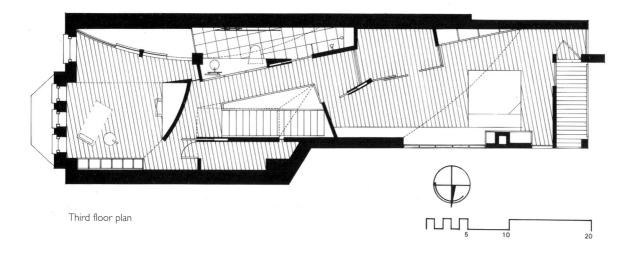

Third floor plan

5   10   20

356

West elevation

Some of the materials used in the master bedroom are lead-coated copper wall-cladding, mahogany and maple cabinets, and a pietra verde limestone countertop.

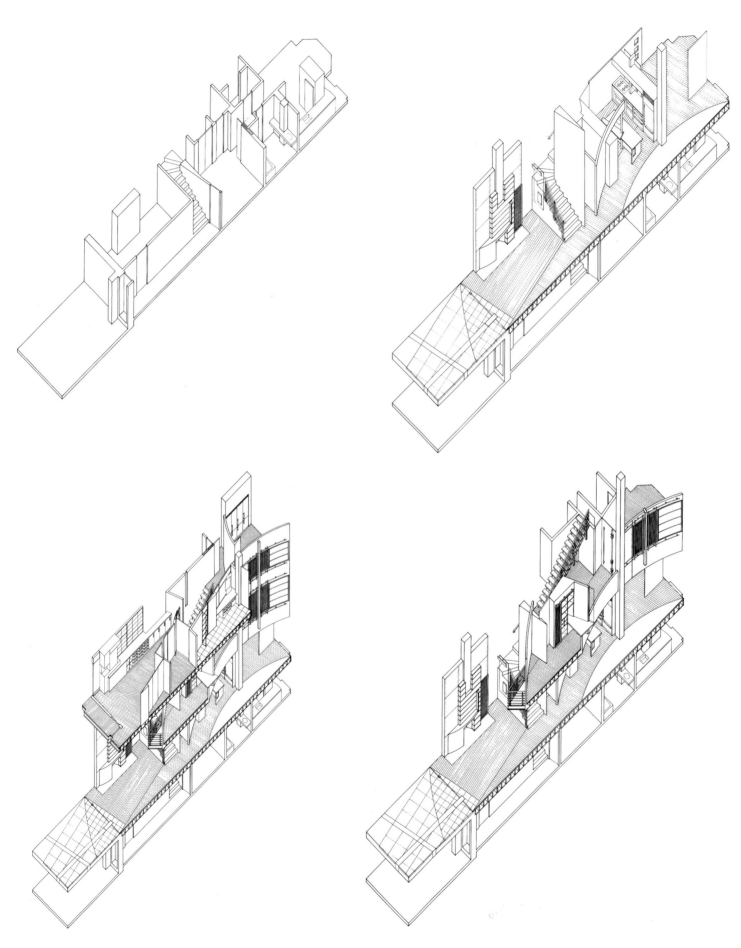

An open well is formed by the repetition in the balcony of a 30-foot-long curved stainless steel plate adorning the kitchen floor. This simple curved opening also helps avoid the typical in-line room arrangement ordinarily dictated by such a long, narrow site.